STAGE A POETRY SLAM

STAGE A POETRY SLAM

Creating Performance Poetry Events

Insider Tips, Backstage Advice, and Lots of Examples

MARC KELLY SMITH

WITH JOE KRAYNAK

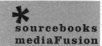

sourcebooks mediaFusion

An Imprint of Sourcebooks, Inc.©
Naperville, Illinois

Published by Sourcebooks MediaFusion, an imprint of
Sourcebooks, Inc.
P.O. Box 4410, Naperville, Illinois 60567–4410
(630) 961–3900
Fax: (630) 961–2168
www.sourcebooks.com

Cataloging-in-Publication data is on file with the publisher.

Printed and bound in the United States of America.
VP 10 9 8 7 6 5 4 3 2 1

CONTENTS

INTRODUCTION

Slams are captivating poetry events that focus an audience's attention on the presentation of poetry that's been composed, polished, and rehearsed for the purpose of being *performed*—very often in a competitive arena. A slam can be a carnival, a pageant, an interactive classroom, a town meeting, a con game, a versified boxing match, and a churchlike revival all rolled into one mind-bending, border-breaking event constructed to electrify and animate the people listening to and watching it, as well as the performers who bring their words, bodies, and voices to life onstage to actuate it.

As you'll learn in the chapters to come, competition is not the solitary heartbeat at the core of the poetry slam, but it has been an important catalyst to its growth. In tournaments around the world *competitive* slam poets battle against one another like wrestlers vying for a championship belt. Poets of all ages and all cultures participate in local, national, and international poetry slam competitions to claim superiority as both poet and performer, and to have their words heard by high energy audiences known to roar approval or stomp their boots in scorn for the poetics they love or pretend to hate.

Where Is Slam?

Poetry slams can be found nearly anywhere—in schools, between office cubicles, at festivals, in bars, at wedding celebrations, at museums, in cultural centers, and even in Laundromats. Performance poets have trained themselves to succeed wherever and in whatever context they're called on to emote—bowling alleys, churches, temples, pool halls, street fairs, commuter trains, discotheques, you name it. The slam's mission has been to throw off the shackles of how and where poetry should be presented. "Try anything and go anywhere" has been the creed. Seek out an audience and compel them to listen. If you can stop bowling balls with a line of verse, you're slammin'.

What the Slam Can Do for You

Slam's primary mission is to garner new audiences for poetry by making it entertaining and accessible. Around the world slams have attracted thousands of new folks to an art form they thought too high-falutin for their tastes. If you're a producer of poetry events or just a lover of poetry and wish to expand attendance at your events, the slam can do that for you. If your programming has become too predictable, too status quo, then slam principles can breathe new life into it. If you're a teacher experiencing difficulty inspiring your students to open poetry texts, the slam can compel those same students to beg you for more to read.

In a nutshell, the slam has made poetry as vital and as popular an art form as any other performing art. For those who become involved in creating shows and performing onstage, slam has the power to transform individuals and build communities. Lost souls, many who have become the best and brightest of the slam tradition, have discovered their voices and built confidence through the slam.

What You Can Do for the Slam

As slam organizer, you're the catalyst who can make it all happen. You set the stage for the poet performers. You generate the buzz that attracts the crowds. You conduct the show as emcee or recruit a suitable personality to keep the show moving forward and the audience engaged and entertained. Without you, slams don't happen.

This book is dedicated to you. Through it, I hope to equip you with the skills to make *your* slam happen. Here, I take you through the process of building your own slam from scratch—locating the right venue; recruiting volunteers; setting the stage, including lighting and sound; lining up performance poets; publicizing your show to raise it to the status of spectacle; and growing your show nationally and internationally.

I wrote this book for everyone who's interested in infusing their community with the energy of performance poetry and breathing new life into an art form that had nearly died. Whether you're a teacher dedicated to drawing students to poetry, an owner of a bar or coffee shop looking to deliver an invigorating form of entertainment to your patrons, or a regular Joe or Josephine determined to liven up your community with something more intellectually stimulating than a wet T-shirt contest, this book is for you.

A NOTE FROM THE PUBLISHER

A few years ago, Sourcebooks MediaFusion was privileged to publish *The Spoken Word Revolution*, edited by Mark Eleveld and advised by Marc Kelly Smith (coauthor of the book you're holding). In the tradition of our book *Poetry Speaks*, which featured historic poets reading their own work, *Spoken Word* brought forth today's vibrant, living world of performed poetry.

While those works included audio CDs bound into the book, today we have the opportunity to bring the world to you online in all its kicking, evolving glory. So we invite you to join the revolution at PoetrySpeaks.com, an emerging home for this vital art form.

You'll find scores of samples, examples, and tracks you can use along with this book for inspiration. Some of the movement's best talent is represented there, plus you'll have the chance to join the community, post your own material, get feedback, maybe even inspire someone else. Come join the revolution and see for yourself at:

www.PoetrySpeaks.com

ACKNOWLEDGMENTS

I would like to thank the slammers around the world for their contributions to this book and to the slam community in general. Special thanks to Mark Eleveld, editor of the *Spoken Revolution* books, and to the folks at Sourcebooks who made this project possible.

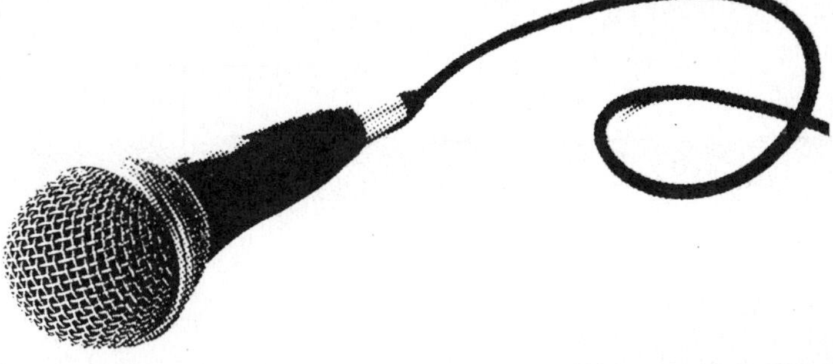

NEXT UP!

Spoken Word Poetry's Long Tradition

Battling Bards

Coming of Age in the 21st Century

Who Inspired This Madness? and Why?

Slam Poetry Goes National

Slam Poetry Goes Global

Slam Poetry Here and Now

If you remember anything, remember...

1
DIGGING THE ROOTS OF SPOKEN WORD POETRY

If you've ever attended an old-school poetry reading (crusty bards droning their precious stanzas to stoic, well-behaved audiences composed of relatives, chums, and students pandering for extra credit), slam poetry might sound crude! *or* (Muse forbid) new! and exhilarating—a cross between an uplifting sermon and a barroom brawl. On whatever side of the coin you flop, know that poetry has a long tradition of being both loud and competitive. In this chapter, I reveal a bit of that history and link it to the principles that continue to fuel slam's growth and evolution.

Slam poets captivate and engage the audience.

Spoken Word Poetry's Long Tradition

Throughout human history, poetry and spoken word arts have been essential to the preservation and celebration of all aspects of the human condition. Every culture has had its poets and oral historians who have witnessed and recounted the intrigues, wanderings, beliefs, desires, tragedies, and joys of the human experience.

Today, nestled in the north woods of Michigan, there's a place called Stone Circle where folks have been gathering around an open fire for several decades to preserve the oral tradition by telling stories and reciting poems as the red sparks fly into the starry summer nights.

> Built by poet Terry Wooten (Terry-Wooten.com), Stone Circle is a triple circle of eighty-eight large boulders located north of Traverse City, Michigan, and designed to capture the atmosphere of ancient cultures that gathered families and community groups to share stories of everyday life and lore. Each summer, it hosts poets, storytellers, and musicians.

In Africa, poets called praise singers, or griots, still carry news from village to village singing their versified headlines just as their ancestors did more than eight hundred years ago.

In Jamaica, dub poets deliver the political news in much the same manner, and in Irish pubs, poets turn their backs on attentive audiences as an act of humility when rhyming out the lyrics and ballads that relate the tests and toils of their Gaelic culture.

Guru Nanak, the sage of the Sikh religion, gathered his flock by reciting divinely inspired poems outside the gates of cities in Pakistan and India to the plucking of his rebab's strings.

Western civilization harkens back to the blind poet Homer, whose epics were composed to be recited aloud, as evidenced by oft-repeated "formulas" like "fleet-footed Achilles" and "when rosy-fingered Dawn appeared." From *Beowulf* to the Bible, literary history is rooted in oral tradition.

Slam poetry carries that tradition forward, encouraging today's poets and performance artists to address the modern human condition by bringing to life (and the spotlight) personal, political, social, and spiritual concerns while knocking the socks off an audience through the artful and entertaining application of performance.

Slam poetry is a term applied to all forms of spoken word poetry composed to be performed in front of a live audience and quite often in a competitive arena. A poetry slam is the actual performance poetry event that usually culminates in a figurative battle between slam poets.

*
for glossary

Battling Bards

In the elitist halls of academia, some literature professors scoff at the notion of performance poetry competitions. They seem to ignore the fact that literary competitions have a long and honorable history. Dionysos, the ancient Greek god of fertility (also believed to be the inventor of wine), watched over his ecstatic worshippers as they drank the blood of animals and danced in an orgiastic frenzy while poet/dramatists—Euripides and Sophocles, to name a famous pair—competed for first prize in festival competitions sponsored by prominent citizens.

Many cultures have used competitive literary events to pique their listeners' interest and improve the quality of their art. In fifteenth-century Japan, samurai-turned-poet Bashō wandered the countryside judging haiku contests, and long before that, his predecessors engaged in contests to collectively compose lengthy poems called *renga*—each poet adding a verse until the renga was complete. The trick was to compose a killer verse that would awe the other poets and challenge the next scribbler to top it with superior verse.

Winter sun rises
To heat the sea rich with words
SlamLaKour speaks

—Marc Smith

Purple sunset gray of wind
Slam here inside, slam in front

—Stef H2K

Under the sun sugar cane flower
Wears its clothes
Pie piled on the horse-car cart

—Samuel "poison" ablancourt

Without hope, I'm in the storm
With hope the wind pulls me

—adjmael halidi

Future is hard to know
Present is hard to catch
There's only past left to remember

—Tilahy

Sun Rebellious with hope
Laughter lives as poetry

—Comrade Fatso

—composed at the SlamLaKour festival on Reunion Island 2008

In the early 1600s, Cervantes mentions poetry contests in his famous work, *Don Quixote:*

...tell me, what verses are those which you have now in hand...If it be some gloss, I know something about glosses, and I should like to hear them; and if they are for a poetical tournament, contrive to carry off the second prize...

At about the same time in Mexico, no doubt influenced by their fellow poets in Spain, hundreds of poets would gather to compete in public poetic jousts called *Justas Literarias* to win awards and fame.

Even in the sacred circles of the high literature elite where the page overshadows the stage, competition is often vicious. Instead of competing for audience approval, poets submit to the private judgment of editors, deans, publishers, and institutions doling out contest awards, grants, publications, and enrollment in MFA (Master of Fine Arts) programs. If you think that's not a competitive arena, think again.

Coming of Age in the 21st Century

Poetry's oral tradition has never come close to drawing a last breath, but it certainly was neglected in America and most of Western Europe during the twentieth century. Some attribute this to New Criticism's grip on literary sensibilities. Others say that mass media and TV drew audiences away from all the performance arts including the elocutionists, troubadours, and concert-hall poets of the late nineteenth and early twentieth centuries.

New Criticism is a formal way of interpreting literature that focuses mainly on the structure and content of the text, ignoring any outside influences, such as the historical and social climate in which the text was written and events in the author's life. New Criticism fostered a more elitist view of poetry and other forms of literature by attempting to make "good taste" the objective.

In the 1950s and '60s the beatniks and hippies rekindled interest in spoken word poetry by reacting to the icy political restrictions of the Cold War era. Allen Ginsberg recited *Howl* at Gallery Six in 1956 long before it appeared in print, and even after *Howl* was published, Ginsberg continued his passionate recitation of it time and time again. (Just how many times did Ginsberg read that poem?!)

The stereotypical images of beatnik poetry readings are stamped on the public psyche to this day. Goatees, bongos, and the swirl of reefer in the air still permeate the collective mind-set of Baby Boomers. Most of us remember news clips of flower children reading poems to National Guard troops while slipping daisies into rifle barrels, and we associate these images with free love and free verse. The poems of Amiri Baraka, Lawrence Ferlinghetti, and even Muhammad Ali, were at the vanguard of a nation in flux during the radical sixties.

Many poets, reporters, and critics of the slam erroneously describe it as an extension of the Beat Generation. It is not. Its roots are more akin to the folk movement of the late fifties and early sixties. It strives to bring together divergent communities, not to drop out of society and form a hipster elite as the early beats did.

In the seventies, the raging howl of the sixties was traded in for disco and leisure suits. The poetry boomers born out of the beats and hippies grew up, got jobs, and enrolled their kids in good schools. But in less fortunate neighborhoods, the new word revolution was remixing music and language and stuffing it with radicalized meaning. The culture of that revolution is hip-hop—underprivileged kids break-dancing on street corners, scratching LPs, and laying down lyrics in a circle, rapping.

Cops came and kicked them off the corners, so they started parties, spun records, scratched the grooves, blended the music, and rapped over it. What began with a few hundred black and Latino kids in neglected neighborhoods of New York City has become a worldwide entertainment industry. It was a music thing, but spoken word fueled it.

By the early 1980s, traditional poetry events had diminished to sporadic, self-absorbed, nonadventures cramped uncomfortably in bookstore aisles and attended by a handful of insular followers. Even the most prominent poets could hardly attract more than a few dozen devotees who politely, though dispassionately, applauded each poem in a series of monotone presentations that barely shifted in style from one muttering to the next, even when the subject changed dramatically from God to war to heartbreak.

In those days, open mics, the come-one-come-all poetic forums, had no legitimate audience whatsoever. They were narcissistic displays of poets reading to poets, eager to hear only themselves, quick to exit after uttering their last lines.

This ineffective approach to the presentation of poetry is what the slammers in Chicago reacted to, sought to change, and did.

The Chicago Poetry Ensemble (a handful of dedicated poets) was the foundation of slam's early experimentation. They were on point in a hostile environment. They were criticized and scoffed at by the academic insiders and the hipper-than-thou outsiders for daring to perform poetry like actors or clowns or singers. Maybe, they were just too naïve to know that they were doing what they shouldn't be doing: what the establishment found distasteful and what the nouveau rebels thought too entertaining. All that matters now is that they did it and formed the roots of what was to become slam.

Who Inspired This Madness? and Why?

Performance poetry as we know it today was the brainchild of yours truly—Marc Kelly Smith (*So What!*), ringmaster of the blue-collar intellectuals and eccentrics who crammed into Chicago's Get Me High Jazz Club on Monday nights from November 1984 to September 1986 for a wide-open poetry experiment that spawned the Chicago Poetry Ensemble and evolved into the international poetry slam movement.

> My So What! handle comes from the early days at the Get Me High Jazz Club when it was important to remind everybody taking the stage, including myself, that we were on an equal footing with everyone else.

I was driven by the belief that if poetry were to be performed artfully and with passion it would attract audiences from all sectors of life. And it has.

The Chicago Poetry Ensemble formed the roots of what was to become slam.

The success of Monday nights at the Get Me High led to the creation of a poetry vaudevillian cabaret show called the Uptown Poetry Slam, the original slam. The show debuted on July 20, 1986, at the Green Mill Jazz Club on Chicago's North Side and featured performances by the Chicago Poetry Ensemble and other local poets with flair for the dramatic. It's where the term "poetry slam" was first coined and stamped on the face of performance poetry and later competitive poetry.

We brazen experimenters in this new style of poetic presentation gyrated, rotated, and spewed our words along the bar top, dancing between the bottles, bellowing out the back door, and busking on the street corners, turning uptown Chicago into a rainforest of dripping whispers on one night and into a blast furnace of fiery elongated syllables, phrases, and snatches of script on the next.

Flyer announces one of the first poetry shows at the Get Me High Jazz Club.

Slam Poetry Goes National

In 1990, the first National Poetry Slam (NPS) competition was held in San Francisco as part of the third Annual National Poetry Week Festival. Gary Glazner, the inspired promoter of this first intercity slam greeted the Chicago poets and the San Francisco audience with the verve of a hot dog vendor barking the relish they were about to devour.

Lois Weisburg, the Commissioner of Chicago's Department of Cultural Affairs, was instrumental in making this premiere NPS happen. Under her suggestion, and with the city's financial help, Chicago sent a team of four poets (Patricia Smith, Cin Salach, Dean Hacker, and me) to challenge teams from San Francisco and New York City. Gary recruited a San Francisco team, and Bob Holman, who had just started a slam at the Nuyorican Café in New York, arranged for Paul Beatty to be the sole New York representative.

About three hundred people showed up at the Fort Mason cultural center to check out what this slam stuff was all about—quite a crowd for a poetry reading in those days, even in San Francisco. Plopped down in the first rows with their arms crossed over their chests were sour-faced remnants of the Beat Generation ready to dismiss this Johnny-come-lately "slam thing" as just another desperate gimmick to con people into attending a reading by a group of aspiring nobodies.

The coin was tossed and Chicago chose to spit first. Patricia Smith stepped to the microphone, and by the time she finished, the audience members were off their seats and on their feet roaring approval. Not a sour face could be seen anywhere. Standing ovations cheered on the Chicago team for the rest of the evening. The fire had been brought down from the mountain, and the ignited room knew something important had just happened.

> This is a tenet of slam philosophy: What we do, what we know, what we discover gets passed on from poet to poet, from city to city, from slam to slam, even to our rivals...our competitive enemies.

Slam Poetry Goes Global

The first person to envision an international slam scene was Michael Brown, originally from Chicago and now retired to the coast of Maine. Michael contacted Swedish poet Erkki Lappalainen to create an Olympic-style slam tournament. It never materialized, but through Michael's missionary efforts, slam spread to Sweden, England, and Germany. Closer to home, Canada began staging regular slams in Montreal, Vancouver, Toronto, Winnipeg, and Ottawa.

Canadian teams have participated in the U.S. national slams since 1992. In 2000, Shane Koyczan from Vancouver won the USNPS Individual Slam Championship.

At Roma Poesia in 2002, poet Lello Voce staged the first truly International Poetry Slam on the upper level concourse of a train station in the middle of Rome. Poets from Spain, France, Russia, Germany, England, Italy, and the United States participated. The slammers performed in their native tongues with translations projected on a huge video screen behind them. It was a visual solution to the problem of judging a multilingual slam competition, and it was a complete success. The Italian audiences witnessed and enjoyed the physical performance and the verbal music of various foreign languages without losing the meaning of what was being said.

Today the largest slam communities outside the United States are in France and Germany, but slam is growing exponentially across the globe. Ireland, the UK, Australia, Zimbabwe, Madagascar, Reunion Island, Singapore, Poland, Italy, and even the South Pole have thriving slam communities. The names of organizers and zealots responsible for this growth are too long to list here. (I've included an appendix—Appendix C to be precise—for that.) Their devotion, passion, and belief can never be adequately quantified; their efforts and accomplishments are tens to the power of infinity.

Slam Poetry Here and Now

By some estimates the slam is the largest and most influential social/literary arts movement of our age. Its principles and formats are used by educators at every grade level to spark student interest in poetry and break down the misconception that the poetic arts are for highbrows only. College curriculums include slam as a new literary genre to be studied as both a historical force and performing art. Theatergoers on the Great White Way have witnessed slammers rock the house at the Tony Award winning production *Def Jam Poetry on Broadway*. Festivals around the world include slam events in their programs.

Only time can reveal what lasting contribution slam will have on the world's literary legacy. But what we do know now is that over two thousand slams are operating around the globe attended by thousands and thousands of people. And you don't have to play bongos, don a beret, or hide behind dark glasses to be part of it.

If you remember anything, remember...

- Slam is more than just a competition; it's a global social/literary movement fueled by the passion and energy of thousands of organizers, poets, and audience members.

- The root philosophies and styles of the slam movement were germinated and cultivated at the Get Me High Jazz Club in Chicago by the Chicago Poetry Ensemble of which I was proud to be a member.

- The Uptown Poetry Slam, the one that sparked them all, began on July 20, 1986, at Chicago's Green Mill Jazz Club.

- Slams have gone worldwide and continue to spread as a gift passed on from poet to poet, venue to venue, and culture to culture.

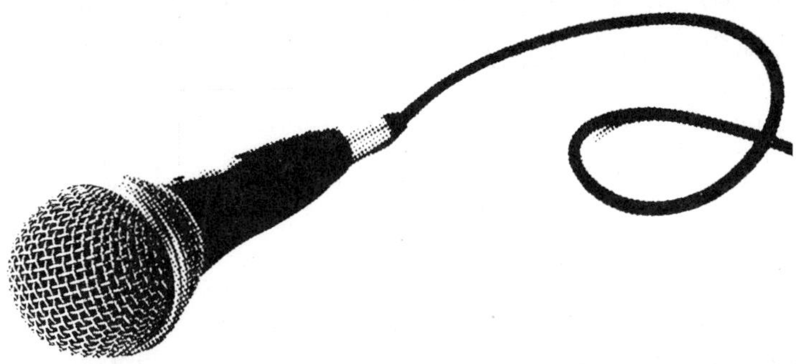

NEXT UP!

The Big Definition of Slam

Poetry and Performance
Staged Bouts for Audience Appeal
"The Points Are Not the Point"

Sowing the Seeds of Slam

Striving for the Best of Both Worlds
Relearning the Art of Listening
Boo! Hiss! Audience with Attitude
Other Strategies Audiences Employ

Who's the Best and Who Cares

Performance Poet as Audience Servant
"As Dr. Willie Used to Say"

Behind the Slam Curtain

Breaking Down the Color (and Collar) Barriers
The Culture of Democracy

If you remember anything, remember...

2 SOAKING IN THE SPIRIT OF SLAM

Stumble into any bar or coffee shop during a *poetry slam,* and you'll witness poets slinging words Out Loud! to win the adulation of an audience and/ or the high scores of judges. You might think that's all there is to it, but if you stick around and listen, you'll discover that a poetry slam isn't just high-volume reading or a heated head-on competition.

To dispel the misconceptions of what slam is or is not and to steep you in its root spirit so that you don't miss out on the best that slam can offer, this chapter highlights the most important tenets of the movement. Here, you'll discover that the "points are not the point." The point is poetic performances that connect to and compel an audience to listen.

The Big Definition of Slam

So if it isn't just a poetry reading and it isn't just a competition, what is it?

A *Poetry Slam* (as the introduction warns) is a word circus, a school, a town meeting, a playground, a sports arena, a temple, a burlesque show, a revelation, a mass guffaw, holy ground, and possibly all of these mixed together. Slam poetry is performance poetry. It's the marriage of a text to its artful presentation onstage to an audience that has permission (and perhaps the responsibility) to talk back. The audience is the primary judge of the quality of the poetry and its presentation.

You hardly ever miss the point at a poetry slam, and if you do, just stand up and holler "Huh?!"

Poetry and Performance

When most people hear the word "poetry," they routinely visualize blocked out stanzas on a page—a text. After all, for the past two hundred–plus years, the printed word has reigned supreme. Poets in print could win Pulitzers—or even a Nobel Prize; a poet screaming award-worthy verse on a street corner in New York could maybe win a night in the slammer.

But if, by default, you found yourself seated in the front row of a poorly ventilated auditorium listening to that Pulitzer Prize–winning poet recite the best of his works, you might be sorely disappointed. Time and time again, the crème de la crème of the printed page have displayed no interest in *performing,* or even a faint desire to add a little inflection to drive home a hot metaphor. They smugly drone on like dust-caked ceiling fans.

Slam strives to invigorate poetry by giving as much weight to the performance as it does to the text. At a poetry slam, a lighthearted scrap of doggerel performed passionately can prove stronger than a superbly crafted villanelle recited by a poet who barely exhibits any signs of life, and by the same token, a fine poem partnered to a fine performance can bring down the rafters.

The goal of performance poetry is to couple the best possible text to the best possible performance—to compose superior poems and perform them with razor-edged precision.

Staged Bouts for Audience Appeal

Standing on the sidelines at your first slam competition witnessing the crowds roar and the poets strut, you might exclaim, "These slammin' poets take themselves way too seriously!" And you'd be right. But hang for awhile and you'll discover that the competition is not the be-all and end-all of slam poetry. It's window dressing. The tournaments, the battles, the bouts are merely, yet importantly, a theatrical device: a mock battle intended to stoke the innate competitive fires, encourage crowd participation, and pump some entertaining fuel into an evening of poetry, interaction, and camaraderie.

When the poetry is compelling and the performances inspired, no matter who nabs the top prize, all involved—the slammers, the organizers, and the audience—walk away winners.

"The Points Are Not the Point"

"...The point is poetry."

This adage, coined by slam poet and organizer Allan Wolf of Asheville, North Carolina, is often repeated at the commencement of slam competitions around the world to remind us that competing in a poetry slam is not about getting the highest score, walking away with a pocketful of cash, or trying to fill a trophy case. The true goal is...to inspire people from all walks of life to listen to poetry, appreciate and respect its power, and ultimately to take the stage and perform their own original works.

The competitive aspect of slam poetry has succeeded at achieving this goal. Slam attracts droves of people, some of whom swore off poetry in high school and college and most are shocked to discover that they actually like it, or at least like some of it.

PSI, the national nonprofit organization representing a large portion of the slam community, makes no mention of "competition" in its mission statement. Its mandate is to promote the awareness of and interest in *performance* poetry, not *competitive* poetry.

Sowing the Seeds of Slam

As I said earlier, the seeds of slam were sown in the womb of the Get Me High Jazz Club (see Chapter 1) on the near northwest side of Chicago, in a beaten-down section of the city that is now, decades later, one of the slickest places to see and be seen in.

The ill-bred poets of the Get Me High adopted and lived by the following principles:

- The poet on the stage is no more important than the listening audience.
- Performing poetry is an art, as much an art as crafting the poetic text itself.
- If you're speaking onstage you have an obligation to do it well; after all, you're competing with all other forms of entertainment.
- And as poet philosopher Wendell Berry instructs us, poetry is not to glorify the poet, but rather to celebrate the community around the poet.

These principles do not seem outrageous today, but in 1984 they were radical. The "establishment poets" declared through their upturned noses that performance cheapened poetry; the *true* poet lets the words, however flat and mumbled off the page, do all the work. But as time has shown, performance actually strengthens poetry's appeal.

Striving for the Best of Both Worlds

Early slammers groomed their texts for performance by red-penciling out abstractions and obscurations and substituting vibrant, concrete language, pertinent themes, and vivid imagery complemented and supported by the most genuine, precise, and powerfully expressed performances they could muster. Their goal was to *communicate,* and if the room's response was poor, they reworked the text, polished the performance, and gave it another sounding when the next opportunity rolled around.

Sometimes they produced sparkling gems; many times they comically shredded a failed poem onstage to the roar of the edifying crowd. They learned the craft and style of performance poetry by trial and error.

Relearning the Art of Listening

The audience learned, too. At a poetry slam, you don't sit at a table with a text in front of your down-focused eyes following along as the poet drips and drabs his words. You lock your line of sight on the poet and tune in to what she's saying and how you're hearing it.

Many of us have forgotten what it is to really listen. We've become visual, video-based, text-based, bar-code-reading junkies. We skim newspapers for headlines, zone out in front of TV screens, play video games for entertainment, and punch out hasty text messages via email and instant-messaging programs.

Gone are the days when the populous pressed its ear to a radio speaker for scratchy fast-breaking, world-shaking news or to hear the Shadow eek through a dark doorway on *Mystery Theater*. Gone are the days when students were expected to recite the classics from memory.

Attending poetry slams gives folks a chance to practice the art of listening, to appreciate and comprehend the richness of our language and the inventiveness of performing wordsmiths. After you've ingested a few slams, you might even notice that you hear more of what everyone has to say in other areas of your life.

Boo! Hiss! Audience with Attitude

The death toll of most poetry readings doesn't ring; it politely pats its paws together to form golf applause in response to the droning monotone of a pedantic, stunningly pompous poet boring the universe with his obscure allusions and endless meandering of self-indulgent observations gleaned from his morning journal.

At most slams such poets had better pull on their thickest rhino hide and get ready to duck. Slam audiences are allowed, encouraged, and sometimes prompted to be brutally honest, to react and respond to what they like and dislike. And they're not stupid.

Audience participation is a key ingredient in the slam recipe. It's the yeast that makes a slam crowd rise to its feet and roar. It takes time to convince a body poetic that it's okay to talk back and get a little rowdy, but once they taste the nectar, they never go back to their hand-sitting, tongue-biting ways.

At the Green Mill, the first sign of trouble is finger-snapping. No, that's not dig-me-daddy-o finger snapping; it's more akin to whistling at a bull fight or the rattle of a snake that's about to strike. If the snapping doesn't clue in the poet that something has gone awry, folks start stomping their feet. When all else fails, they groan like grizzlies—a low, nasty, threatening groan.

Seasoned slam audiences have mastered some specialized control measures. One of the most playful is the feminist hiss, which traditionally was used to gently slap a male poet down for using one too many sexual references in a lonely-hearts poem. Nowadays, audiences use the feminist hiss for just about anything a man does as soon as he steps onstage.

Guess-the-rhyme is another popular game. If a particular poet's rhymes are all too predictable, someone in the audience chimes in by announcing the rhyming word just as it trickles out of the poet's mouth. It's great fun to watch the poet's face when nine out of ten of his hard-sought rhymes are guessed and shouted in unison with his recitation.

Other Strategies Audiences Employ

Around the world slam rituals give the audience a voice and permission to add that voice to the performances they experience. In Jerusalem, slammers serve up their poems onstage as fodder for an open discussion by audience members about the merits and failings of the poem. Then the slammer presents an edified version of the poem and receives a score from the judges who've heard both the poem and the discussion.

In Wiesbaden, Germany, the entire audience scores the performances on ballots passed out at the beginning of the evening: one to five for content, one to five for performance. Included at the bottom of the ballot is a space for comments and criticisms.

The rituals adopted by local slam events nurture and encourage audience participation and are essential to a show's success.

Honest and immediate feedback has enabled slammers to grow as performers and polish their art into highly effective modes of communication. Without a backdrop of honest audience interaction, it's not a slam.

Who's the Best and Who Cares

Throughout history, societies have placed their best poets, authors, and artists on lofty pedestals. They might have scorned and starved them during their lifetimes, but at some point (often after their demise) the masses honored and glorified them.

Placing artists and performers on pedestals isn't an unwarranted and unjust thing to do—assuming all artists of equal caliber have the same opportunity to compete for the pecking-order honors. Problems arise, however, when a particular group of patrons and critics monopolize art and agree on arbitrary sets of rules that prevent other gifted creators from having a shot at the golden goose.

As Five Man Electrical Band sang in the 1970s in their hit song "Signs," "Sign said you got to have a membership card to get inside. Uh!" In the world of slam the only thing excluded is exclusivity.

Performance Poet as Audience Servant

Slam poetry attempts to dissolve the arbitrary barriers between artist and audience by knocking pomposity off its perch and making poets recognize their humble yet noble role—as artistic servants to their culture and community. Slam poets learn early that they had better be tuned into their audience's sensibilities to have any hope of surviving their stay onstage, let alone winning a competition.

In the poet-audience relationship, the crowd is the standoffish mate waiting to be wooed by the poet. The poet dances his words in a mating ritual over the ears and eyes of the soul mate audience that listens carefully—ready to provide the honest feedback the poet needs to sharpen his or her skills.

Sometimes the feedback is encouraging. Other times, it sends the poet scurrying back to his desk in the dark corner of his dimly lit den to practice, rewrite, and practice again before returning to the footlights to renew his wooing performance.

> The best slam poets know that they are audience servants, not sycophants. One of the most disgusting sites at a poetry slam is a poet who knowingly grovels for high scores or audience approval. The poet should serve the audience not only by entertaining its members but also by challenging them. The line is very thin, but performance poets who successfully straddle that line turn in brilliant performances.

"As Dr. Willie Used to Say"

For Years Bob Holman, New York's first slam guru, introduced every slam competition at the Nuyorican Café with the following versified preamble rendering his take of slam's purpose:

> As Dr. Willie used to say,
> We are gathered here today
> because we are not gathered
> somewhere else today, and
> we don't know what we're doing
> so you do—the Purpose of SLAM!
> being to fill your hungry ears
> with Nutritious Sound/Meaning Constructs,
> Space Shots into Consciousness
> known hereafter as Poems, and
> not to provide a Last Toehold
> for Dying Free Enterprise #&@% 'em
> for a Buck'em Capitalism'em. We disdain
> competition and its ally war

and are fighting for our lives
and the spinning
of poetry cocoon of action
in your dailiness. We refuse
to meld the contradictions but
will always walk the razor
for your love. "The best poet
always loses" is no truism of SLAM!
but is something for you
to take home with you like an image
of a giant condor leering over
a salty rock. Yes, we must destroy
ourselves in the constant
reformation that is this very moment,
and propel you to write the poems
as poets read them, urge you
to rate the judges as they trudge
to their solitary and lonely numbers,
and bid you dance or die between sets.

His humorous and challenging declaration of slam's purpose is rooted deep in the soil of slam's original intent.

Behind the Slam Curtain

Center stage focus brightly illuminates the poet/performers, but slam reaches far beyond those in the spotlight, indeed, beyond the walls of any particular venue. It encompasses all the forces involved in staging a show, including the emcee, the host, the ticket takers, the volunteers who pass out flyers promoting the event, and all those who work on the national and international levels to serve the slam community. More important than any individual performer or event, slam is a community of organizers who have discovered a dynamic way of presenting poetry aloud onstage in full public view, enabling its

Bob Holman performs from a fire escape to slammers arriving in San Francisco for the 1993 NPS.

passion, wisdom, and beauty to be experienced with total impact.

Breaking Down the Color (and Collar) Barriers

At about the same time as another famous Chicagoan, Reverend Jesse Jackson, was forming his Rainbow Coalition, the slam community was forming its own *apolitical* rainbow coalition. Visit any national poetry slam competition, and you'll see an astonishing mosaic of diversity. Men and women of all ages, all races and nationalities, all socio-economic brackets, and from every occupational niche of society gather together at these events to share their poetry, their performances, and the joy of creating and being part of the slam family.

Sure, you'll see some healthy competition and some passionate arguments. You might even see a scuffle or an all-out brawl—every crowd has a couple of people who like to be contrary for contrary's sake, especially in a wide open forum. But for the most part, the slam is a grand (if at times dysfunctional) family of poetry lovers from all walks of life getting along and sharing in the excitement—aging hippies, young Goths, burly construction workers, leather-clad bikers, button-down office types, you name it.

The only prerequisite for belonging to the slam family is a sincere desire to enjoy and promote performance poetry.

The Culture of Democracy

The slam community has no grand, high, exalted mystic ruler, no dictator, nobody handing down fixed mandates on how to run local competitions, write poetry, or structure a performance. Each poetry slam and slammaster is autonomous, free to call her own shots. Each show maker decides how she wishes to run her slam. Each slam follows its own rules, rituals, and regulations. Most adhere to the majority of the principles discussed throughout this book, but only by choice, not because they are compelled to do so by some higher authority.

If you remember anything, remember...

- Slam poetry is the remarriage of the art of performing with the art of writing poetry. The goal of performance poetry is to couple the best possible text to the best possible performance.

- When you're in the audience, listen carefully, and be ready to react to the performer by showing your approval or disdain.

- Slam poets should serve the audience without groveling for high scores or pandering to mass appeal.

- The slam organization is democratic; the community welcomes people from all walks of life.

- Remember what Dr. Willie and Allen Wolfe said: "the best poem (may) always lose" but "the points are not the point, the point is poetry."

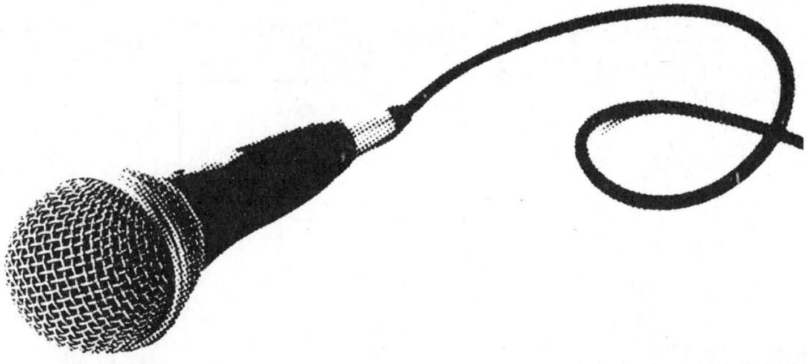

NEXT UP!

It's a Game, Stupid!

A Familiar Format

The First Slam Competition

Who Says Who Wins?

The Basic Rules of Slam Engagement

Perform Your Own Work

Three Minutes Is All We Can Stand

No Props, Costumes, Trombones, or Other Carry-On Luggage

Scoring: 0 to 10 (or Down to Minus Infinity)

Make the Process Fun

Signing 'Em Up

Picking the Judges

Alternative Styles of Judging

Famous Slam Disclaimers

The Mean Chicago Rules

The Official Emcee Spiel Used at the National Poetry Slams

It's Your Thing, Do What You Want to Do...To a Point

Slams Are Open to All

All Styles, Forms, and Subject Matter Are Welcome

The Prize Is Not the Point

The All-Important Audience Should Always Be in Control

If you remember anything, remember...

3 SLAM COMPETITION—RULES, REGULATIONS, AND OTHER FORMALITIES

Competition may not be the core aesthetic of the slam movement, but it has been a major factor in its spread. This is easy to explain. Competition is basic to the human spirit and an integral part of our daily lives and history. It identifies ability and celebrates achievement. And it's fun to watch. Who doesn't enjoy booing a judge, cheering a victorious hero, or sympathizing with an unjustly defeated friend?

Yet, slam competition is only a means to an end—a way to get people excited about poetry, encourage poet-performers to write well, perform

Slam judges chosen from the audience determine what's "best."

brilliantly, and gather into focus a community of people who love the sound of words, the notions they convey, and the emotions they evoke.

This chapter hands you the basic rules, regulations, procedures, and ethics that govern most slams. Of course, you don't need to be a certified slam judge to enjoy a poetry slam (assuming there is such a thing as a certified slam judge), but knowing what's going on helps you get more out of the ballyhoo. More importantly, if you decide to host a show that sends a team to a national slam, you'll need to know this stuff.

It's a Game, Stupid!

In the fervor of competition, many slam poets forget that a slam contest is not a serious determination of who's the best poet or performer. When they react furiously to a low score or bask too long in the glory of a perfect 10, they forget that most of what goes on at a slam is arbitrary—a subjective concoction with unavoidable biases. By what objective criteria can you compare a sonnet to a rant, or a seventeen-syllable haiku to a full three minutes of rap laced with pop images and slick jokes? How can judges, picked randomly from a rowdy unlettered crowd, be seen as an authentic testimony to a poet's value?

Remember, the contest is a theatrical device; it's not meant to be the litmus test of a performance or text. It's a natural drama. Everybody in the moment of the drama wonders who will win, who will get the high score, and who will walk away ten bucks richer. A half hour later, most have forgotten the numbers, but hopefully not the words.

Try this: Go into a restaurant with a friend, sit down at a table, and start arm-wrestling. Bet you'll attract a lot of attention before you're asked to leave. Natural drama draws focus but not without consequences.

A Familiar Format

People listen more intently during a slam competition because it follows a sporty format everyone recognizes—the slammer's up, the pitch comes, a swing, a strike, a stolen simile, a home run, a diving metaphor that saves the game. When a slammer takes the mic, it's batter up, face-off, jump ball. When he speaks, it's the stance and swing, slap the puck, dribble and shoot. When the scores go up, it's the formal acknowledgement of what the audience might have already decided. "This dude didn't know what he was saying or how to say it." Strike three. Or "She was sensational! I wanna buy her book." Grand slam! Swish! Score! Like most sporting events, everybody has an opinion about what should have happened and who should have done what when. That's what keeps them involved up until the last syllable is uttered.

The First Slam Competition

The very first slam competition occurred at the Green Mill on the third (or was it the fourth?) week of the Uptown Poetry Slam's opening run. (No one can remember for sure.) It was an afterthought, an in-the-moment addition to the show, filler for the final act.

Al MacDougal, a merchant marine working on the ore boats that navigate the Great Lakes was the first slam champion. Mary Shen Barnidge, a freelance theater critic, was his last challenger in a king-of-the-hill contest that lasted (as myth has it) nine rounds. Al had successfully defended the hill from eight other opponents, but Mary knocked him off his pile of eight wins with her Dionysos poem.

> The refrigerator chilled twelve bottles of wine,
> And four bottles of poppers lined up neatly in the egg tray.
> The music thundered, making the walls shiver deliciously.
> The main hall was a sea of masks:
> Gold masks, emerald and sapphire masks, black dominos,
> Masks with refraction-lenses that shot prismatic darts
> into every corner,

Skeleton masks, wolf masks, unicorn masks, android masks,
False eyelashes like cilia, burnished wigs like
gorgon's hair,
Masks with mirrors into which one looked to see
himself reflected back.
It was the kind of party where Dionysos would be welcome.
–from "Dionysia" by Mary Shen Barnidge

But the audience raged against the imbalance of awarding Mary the $10 prize for a single winning poem when Al had won the first eight. In the end, Al got the money and bought Mary's drinks for the rest of the evening.

Mary doesn't remember it that way. She swears she wasn't slated to take on Al until weeks after his first slam victory, and then he didn't show up to defend his title. If we knew back then that we were making history, we might have downed less beer and recorded the details of these early events. Ah well.

Who Says Who Wins?

That first competition was determined by audience applause. It took a few months of haphazard experimentation—slams judged by holding up hands, by screaming and not clapping, by clapping without screaming, by stomping of feet—to arrive at the general rule that *competitions should be judged on a point system by judges selected randomly from the audience.* It's still an arbitrary system, but this method elicits less commotion and focuses the boos on the hapless judges rather than on the emcee and organizers.

Rules are important to the structure of any competition. Baseball has nine innings; basketball, two timed halves; and yachting, one long sail. Regulations on structure and procedure frame an event into a digestible

Scoring is more art than science.

dramatic experience. Individual behavior is controlled by parameters set for the benefit of those who play and those who watch—no spitballs, no cork bats, no clipping, no plagiarism. They promote sportsmanlike behavior, keep down the fistfights, and give everybody something to complain about. Rules are meant to create a fair playing field for all participants. And in the slam the rules are also created to be questioned; after all, it's a passionate arena of free speech.

Over the years individuals and teams have tested and exploited the loopholes and gray areas in the rules governing national poetry slams. Sometimes this has led to constructive restructuring of events. Sometimes it's been plain cheating. The spirit of the rules is what is most important. Everyone knows that gray areas exist in the interpretation of the rules, but the slam community encourages participants not to exploit the gray areas for their own personal gain.

The Basic Rules of Slam Engagement

Rules vary from slam to slam, and they should. Each locale needs to adopt the regulations that are most agreeable and entertaining for their specific audience. It's art, not robotics. Be creative. Devise your own format. Establish your own rituals. Follow the basic rules (listed below) to get started, but feel free to modify or scrap whatever doesn't work for your particular show.

- Perform your own work.
- Perform in three minutes or less.
- No props or costumes.
- Scores range from 0.0 to 10.0 using one decimal place to avoid ties.

The following sections examine each of these in glorious detail.

Perform Your Own Work

Most slams encourage and require poets to perform their own work. The rule's intent is obvious: to discourage plagiarism and maintain a level playing field. It simply wouldn't be fair for a novice to pit her first poetic creation against someone performing the great works of Gwendolyn Brooks or Langston Hughes. This rule also encourages young writers to test their ideas and writing skills, opens the doors to poetic innovation, and gives each performer a sounding board for his or her free voice and unfettered emotions.

Performers break this rule all the time—sometimes deceitfully, sometimes with the permission of the audience, and sometimes because a particular poetry slam focuses on the works of famous poets.

Three Minutes Is All We Can Stand

Prior to the slam it was not unusual for a poet to tax an audience's patience with a fifteen-minute poem of questionable aesthetic value. Stage hogs, who cared little about the people upon whom they inflicted their words or the other poets waiting to read, would drain every ounce of enthusiasm from an audience and kill any chance for those who followed to succeed.

The Three-Minute rule put a limit on how much bad verse a poet could spew before the hook appeared in the wings to yank him out of the spotlight. It also became the basic time unit of the competition itself. It's the "at bat"—you get three minutes to make your hit happen. And for most poets that's more than enough time to score big or crawl back to the dugout.

No Props, Costumes, Trombones, or Other Carry-On Luggage

Here's another rule that is often broken for the sheer thrill of breaking it. The No Props rule was initiated during the planning phase of the 1990 National Poetry Slam.

Most of the shows mounted at the Green Mill by the Chicago Poetry Ensemble had employed props, music, and costumes. The Uptown Poetry Slam is designed to be a multimedia cabaret of poetic arts combined with other performing arts that stretches the boundaries of what is considered acceptable at a poetry event.

However, when discussing what might happen at the first major national competition, the Chicago Slam Committee decided to rule out the use of props and music. "What if someone brings a ten-piece orchestra onstage? Or poodles? How will we get them on and off stage without messing up the rhythm of the show? How can you judge an orchestra against a solo poet reciting a villanelle?"

It was somewhat of a tourniquet on the creative juices but it has saved many an organizer the nightmare of exploding cabbages, rolling bath tubs, and six-foot submarine sandwiches. All of which have found their way into poetry performances at special slam competitions staged for the pure joy of breaking the rules.

Scoring: 0 to 10 (or Down to Minus Infinity)

Few slams play by the "mean" Chicago rules that allow the judges to score into the minus numbers. That's a shame, because audiences love when offensive guys and gals get crushed and the good fellas garner a 10.

The 0 to 10 scoring system is fairly universal. At national poetry slams, five judges score each performance, the top and bottom scores are dropped, and the sum of the remaining three represents the "score." In other words, a perfect score is 30 points.

> As the evening wears on, slam scores tend to drift higher. This universal phenomenon known as "score creep" makes it clear that the judges' scores are not entirely objective. Performing last often is enough to tip the scales in favor of a particular performer.

Some slams require the judges to score the poetry and the performance separately: 1 to 5 for performance and 1 to 5 for text. Some score by holding up roses. Some determine the winner by audience applause, which can sound different depending on where you sit. Some have secret ballots. The more involved an audience is in the judging, the more entertaining the show.

Make the Process Fun

People who take themselves too seriously are bores; they usually end up talking to themselves or painting a target on their backs. Overly serious slam competitions can produce the same effect on an entire audience. Use the competition to heighten your show's drama, not flatten it. Generate excitement and entertainment by creating rituals and ceremonies that answer the following questions: Who's going to judge? How? What are the rules? How many bouts? How are contestants chosen? What do they win? The following sections will help guide you.

Signing 'Em Up

Most slams sign up contestants on a first come, first served basis. At the Green Mill, the doorman handles the sign-up board, which consists of six to ten slips of blank paper taped to a poster board. Sign your name on one of them and you're in the slam. Up to a point, it's a case of "the more the merrier."

Part of my ritual schtick at the Green Mill has been to give nicknames to regular slammers: Haiku Joe, Boa Bill, The Body Language Poet, and The Grand Dame of Doom. Most of the time, the poets play along. They appreciate the color the nicknames give to their onstage personas. Many slammers have nicknamed themselves: Wammo, Boogie Man, and The Wire.

Some slams sign up contestants weeks in advance on tournament charts. Some require slammers to provide bios and slam stats—number of performances, where they've previously performed, and so on. Some charge a nominal entry fee to discourage last-minute napkin scribblers who may have imbibed too much and are bent on embarrassing themselves onstage. However you choose to obtain or select your contestants, do it in a fashion that gives the audience a profile of who's up there laying their words on the line.

Picking the Judges

As I stated above, slam hosts traditionally pick three to five judges randomly from the audience, give them cards and markers, and instruct them to score each poem/performance on a scale from 1 to 10, paying equal attention to text and presentation.

Variations on this method are abundant. Feel free to modify it as you wish, with the goal of generating more fun, surprise, and suspense. But be careful not to slow the pace of the show by making the process overly complicated. Here are some dos and don'ts:

- Do keep the judges in clear view of the scorekeepers and emcees for speedy retrieval of the numbers, but DON'T seat the judges close together. Spread them out across the front of the room in prominent positions near the stage so the audience can watch and react to their scoring. "OH MY GOSH! I can't believe that guy gave my little sister a minus four!"

- Do get bio info about the judges. When introducing the judges, have the emcee turn it into a ritual by gathering and embellishing on biographical information about the judges. *Where is she from? Is it his first time at the slam? What does she do for a living? Is he here just because he heard that smart chicks like slam?* Judges are characters in the slam play. Flesh out those characters and make them colorful.

Adding up three scores takes just the right amount of time to clear the palate between slammers. When you use five judges, you usually knock out the high and low score, but it slows the pace of the show. Waiting for more than five judges to hold up their cards and tallying more than five numbers can drag the slam momentum to a plodding yawn.

- Do use celebrity judges—maybe. If they're truly celebrities and have playful, charismatic personalities, they can spark things up quite a bit. But if they take their judging roles too seriously or are just plain drips, beware! A barfly who gets booed for his bogus scoring provides more action than prissy judges doing a "proper" job.

- Do judge by committee—if it works. Judging by committee can result in too much consultation and dead air while you wait for the consensus score. If you can hustle them to deliver in a timely fashion, it can be great. Give a table of judges a group name and personality. "Okay. And now the score from the Greeks! And where's the score from Freaks?" If a committee takes too long, ignore their score, or set a time limit—"The Lawyer Committee has 10 seconds to come up with a number, or they'll need to rise and deliver a group apology—in iambic pentameter."

Alternative Styles of Judging

The more an audience participates—the more stuff you make them do, the more memorable the evening becomes for them. Here are some examples:

- **Rose battle.** In Bonn, Germany, everyone in the room receives a rose when they arrive. At the conclusion of the first round of slammers they hold the roses over their heads when their favorite poet's name is announced. The raised roses are counted, and the poets with the three highest rose counts go on to the final round. After the poems have been presented in the final round, the poets are brought up to the stage one by one, and the audience tosses the roses to their desired champion. The slammer with the biggest bouquet is declared the Rose Winner.

- **Pass the bucket.** As a supplement to numerical judging, several slams pass buckets with the names of the competitors pasted on them to collect tribute from the patrons who place bucks in the buckets for the slammers they think deserve their support. It doesn't determine the official winner, but a bucketful of cash always generates a little excitement.

In Northern California, organizers use many different formats: haiku, limerick, freestyle battles. In the dreaded "Canadian Bucket Match," two poets perform while two buckets are passed around. The audience votes by pitching money into their favorite poet's bucket. The poet with the most money wins. Other changes in rules include ballots instead of scores, themed slams, different time limits, even returning to the head-to-head bout format from which slam originated.
—Charles Ellik, Berkley slammaster

- **Applause-o-meter.** When judging by audience applause, emcees often turn themselves into human sound sensing machines, using their arms like the pointers on a gas gauge to display for all to see the levels of applause they're hearing. Some slammasters have gone as far as purchasing actual sound-sensitive devices and jury-rigging them into slam meters with flashing lights that respond to the hoots, hollers, and claps. Unfortunately, these machines register all audio feedback—cheers and boos—equally.

When devising an alternative judging style, be sure that it has a simple structure, a lighthearted nature, and some visual element that the entire audience can watch and enjoy.

Famous Slam Disclaimers

- Slam organizers from early on have tried to express to newcomers that "all's not fair" at the slam—that it's entertainment. Trying to determine whose poem and performance is truly the best through a slam competition is absurd. Remember, "points are not the point." To drive this home, many slammasters and show hosts have created rituals and liturgies that announce these facts of life at the beginning of their shows. (See Bob Holman's disclaimer in Chapter 2.) This ensures that the audience approaches the event with the proper perspective.

The Mean Chicago Rules

For the past two decades I've begun every Sunday night at the Green Mill slam with the same spiel:

> At the Uptown Poetry Slam you, the audience, are always in control. If you like something, you cheer madly. [The audience cheers.] You would think that that positive reinforcement is what has made the slammers strong, but you'd be wrong. It's the other stuff that has. If you don't like what you hear you can express yourselves in one of several manners. If you don't like it a little bit, you snap your fingers. [The audience snaps.] That's not dig-me-daddy-o, those guys are dead and gone. This is a new regime. If you don't like it a little bit more, stomp your feet. [They stomp.] If it's god awful bad, you groan. [Grooooooooooaaaaaaaaaaaaaaaaan!]
> There's also the feminist hiss. [Hissssssssssssssssss] It used to be for when a man got sexist in his poem, but now it's for just about anything a man does as soon as he steps up onto the stage. [They cheer.] After years of being hissed at, the men finally came up with the masculine grunt. [A whimper] That says it all about the masculine grunt.

There's also Guess the Rhyme: If there should happen to be a rhyming poet up here on the stage and you, the audience, can guess the rhyming word before it arrives, you may in unison with the poet say the word and watch his or her face—it's great fun.

Scoring is allowed to go into the minus numbers and the lowest score ever achieved at the Uptown Poetry Slam (or any slam for that matter) is minus infinity.

The Official Emcee Spiel Used at the National Poetry Slams

The official emcee spiel used at the national poetry slams is much more succinct and sounds much more official. Before the start of any national competition, this is what you hear:

"The [National] Slam is a performed poetry competition judged by five members of the audience. Poets have three minutes to present their original work and may choose to do so accompanied by members of their team. The judges will then score the piece anywhere from 0 to 10, evaluating both the poet's performance and the contents of the poem. Points will be deducted for violating the time limit. The highest combined team score wins the bout. We encourage the audience to let the judges know how you feel about the job that they are doing. We exhort the judges to remain unswayed by crowd pressure. We are sure that the poetry will be worth your attention."

It's Your Thing, Do What You Want to Do... To a Point

Organizers at the local level who take on the burden of creating slams have every right to construct shows in a manner that best suits their communities. The time, the energy, and don't forget the dough that organizers expend to achieve liftoff deserves admiration and respect. They will initially wonder if the payoff is worth the effort. All will encounter resistance and criticism from friends and foes alike. At this very moment there are slammasters sitting in the darkest corners of bedrooms with their hands gripping their heads mumbling "Why, why, why?"

Organizers of certified slams sanctioned by PSI (Poetry Slam Inc) carry the moniker *slammaster*. He or she is the person producing the show, filling out the paperwork connected with PSI membership, and voting at biannual meetings.

So if and when you start a slam, keep in mind that it's your show. If folks think it's bogus, let 'em start their own. If they start one and begin drawing audience away from yours, maybe it's time for a little slam self-examination. If not, you're on the right track. Oftentimes two competing slams in the same region or city both thrive. After all, poetry is a big house with many rooms.

However, there are a handful of sacred traditions that define the essential nature of slam. Slams that break with these traditions usually become something other than slam. Here are the main traditions that define and propel the movement.

Slams Are Open to All

Slam is an agent against elitism and exclusivity, open to any and all who walk through the doors. Of course, nobody welcomes a jerk who's bent on using the stage to impose wickedness on the audience. Slam provides everyone with an equal first chance (and often a second, third, and fourth chance) to find a place in the community and on a slam stage.

If a particular slam works for you, great. If it doesn't, try some place else or create your own slam. Slams can be as different as night and day, but all slams should be open to all poet performers.

In its two-decade history of over a thousand performances, only a handful of poets have been banned from the Uptown Poetry Slam. One for burning a flag onstage and causing a fire hazard, one for equating a woman's body to an automobile in a particularly offensive way, and one for threatening the audience with a knife. Open doesn't mean stupid. Don't let a creep kill your show or harm anybody attending it.

All Styles, Forms, and Subject Matter Are Welcome

Sonnets, haiku, pantoums, villanelles, raps, rants, ballads, limericks... you name it, and it's been performed on a slam stage. Love, religion, politics, body odors, taxes, dog poo—it's been done. Anything and everything is game, but remember, the audience can give it right back. And there are more of them than there are of you.

Dozens of anthologies feature poems that have gained creditably and acclaim on slam stages (see Appendix A). Browse through a few of them and you'll immediately realize the broad range of styles and forms brought to sound and life by slam poets.

The Prize Is Not the Point

Some slams offer major cash prizes to winners. Big buck prizes can draw top shelf contenders and media attention to special slams and annual events. They can also produce major headaches for organizers and cultivate an atmosphere of tension counter to the playfulness and community-building goals slam seeks to achieve.

Traditionally, ongoing weekly, monthly, and quarterly slams offer modest awards to contestants. Ten to fifty bucks, books, CDs, gift certificates, and eligibility to compete for spots on national slam teams are all examples of typical slam prizes.

Individuals and entities that create high profile slam tournaments with eye-popping, mind-blowing prizes beyond the scope and grasp of local organizers are working against the grass roots principles of the slam. Poetry stops being the point; the point becomes *winning* at any cost *the prize.*

The Twinkie prize at the Green Mill was held in high esteem. No, it wasn't a booby prize, it was for the winner! It ranked right up there with the coveted box of macaroni and cheese autographed by the judges. And for many years Big John, the doorman at the Green Mill, offered the Sunday night slam winner Lotto tickets as an alternative to taking the $10. It was called the Big John Scam. In the ten years that Big John ran his scam, nobody ever scratched off more than another free ticket.

The All-Important Audience Should Always Be in Control

Let your audience actively express themselves, not abusively but honestly. Announce the ground rules, and they'll do the rest. If you give them a say, they'll be back to listen again and again. The Green Mill Uptown Poetry Slam has passed its twenty-second year playing to standing room only crowds. Over eighty thousand different people have seen the show. That should be proof enough.

If you remember anything, remember...

- The competitive component of slam poetry is a theatrical tool intended to liven up the show and inspire the poet/performers to do their best.

- Basic slam rules require poets to perform their own work, in three minutes or less, wearing no costumes and using no props, and are scored on a scale from 0 to 10.

- Turn the judging process into an entertaining ritual that puts colorful face on all the onstage personalities.

- At the beginning of each slam event, the emcee typically recites a disclaimer that undercuts the seriousness of the competition and sets a tone for the show.

- To remain true to slam, follow the traditions that define it: Open it to anyone, allow all styles of poetry, the prize is not the point, and give the audience control.

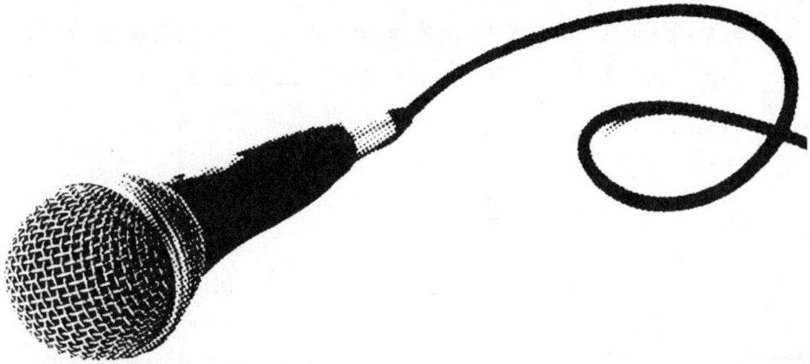

NEXT UP!

Do You Have the Itch?

Taking Inventory—Do You Have What It Takes?

Are You Doing This for Yourself?
Do You Have a Vision?
Do You Have a Support Network?
Do You Have the Time and Energy?
Are You a Show Maker?
Are You as Crazy as the Rest of Us?

Tallying Your Talents and Resources

Been There, Seen That
Been There, Done That

Anticipating the Obstacles Ahead

The Hoity-Toity Establishment
Cash Flow Problems

Shifting Sands—Unforeseen Changes
Pettiness and Social Hostility

If you remember anything, remember...

4 SHOULD I BECOME A SLAMMASTER?

You live or teach in Dullsville, where people go to the mall on Friday nights and stay home on Saturday to watch TV. Nobody ventures outside the box. And the few "fun" things to do can't possibly be considered intellectually stimulating—little league ball games, demolition derbies, and bingo. You have to drive 60 miles to see a live band. The arts community leadership died years ago, and the only ongoing slam is 200 miles away. You may as well be living in a basement at the local cemetery.

Whaaaa! Whaaaa! Whaaaa!

Stop your whining. Drop that remote. Spring out of your recliner and put together your own slam show. ... But wait a minute. Can you do it? Do you have what it takes? If you were to start your own show, what would you be getting yourself into? Well, this chapter will help you answer these questions and decide whether being a slammaster is the life for you.

Do You Have the Itch?

If you've got the itch, you'll know it as sure as if a Mississippi mosquito were sucking on your face. If you attend a slam, and you can't keep the mind chatter from squawking, "This would be a whole lot more interesting, if..." you have the itch. If you're bumping into telephone poles preoccupied with various hypothetical slam scenarios, you've got the itch. If you're sitting at the Clyde Clip Clop Word Fair and can't help but think, "Gee, those cowboy hats and bolos are a nice touch, but I'd add a yodeling competition," you've got the itch. And when you've got the itch, you'd better scratch it, because it ain't goin' away.

Is that a bad thing? Should you be afraid? Heck no, you'll survive. You're going to run full-speed into glass doors, fall off your horse, and kick yourself for being such a damn fool. But none of this matters;

If the slam bug has its incisors in your flank, it's hopeless. You're going to make a difference whether you like it or not.

And how do you go about scratchin' that itch? We'll lasso that question near the end of this chapter. Right now, you need to figure out whether you've got the right stuff to even consider making the move.

Taking Inventory—Do You Have What It Takes?

Before setting out on any journey, most folks take an inventory. Do they have their money, keys, medicine, plane tickets, and toothbrush? The same is true when they decide to embark on any important venture, such as getting married, starting a business, or buying a home. Do they really want to accept a new responsibility? Do they have the requisite resources to succeed or at least survive?

To decide whether you have the drive and resources you need to make your slam show a success, answer the following questions:

- Are you doing this for yourself?

- Do you have a vision?

- Do you have a support network?

- Do you have the time and energy?

- Are you a show maker?

- Are you as crazy as the rest of them slam folk?

Now read the following sections to explore these questions in greater detail.

Are You Doing This for Yourself?

Few, if any of us, are completely selfless individuals. We do what we do because our actions reward us in some way. Maybe they bring us money, give us pleasure, or make us feel appreciated and loved. There's nothing wrong with that, so don't beat yourself up if you're creating a slam primarily because you think it'll be a blast, give you more artistic freedom, and increase your visibility in the slam community.

However, if you're setting out to completely use people for your own benefit, you're in the wrong division of the entertainment industry. The slam has adamantly opposed exploitive personalities and organizations wishing to capitalize on its name, reputation, and collective energies. The movement stands upon the shoulders of thousands of dedicated, service-minded people who have received little or no material return from their vast personal investments of time, money, energy, and emotion. By becoming a slammaster you're joining an extremely passionate group of self-sacrificing idealists.

Go to www.poetryslam.com and click Find a Slam, or head to Appendix C to view the extent of slams and slammasters across the country and around the world.

But you need not be Mother Teresa—unless you really want to be. There's nothing wrong with a dog wagging its own tail. A spot in your slam to do your own work? An opportunity to stretch your performance horizon? A chance to earn a little money and get some respect and attention? Nothing's wrong with that. The conflicts arise when people start getting waaaaaaaaaaay more than they give back and when they consider themselves to be waaaaaaaaaaay more important than they really are—when the tail starts wagging the dog.

Do You Have a Vision?

Starting a slam affords you the opportunity to *create,* not just pour your soul into a prefab slam mold. Take the basic form and explore. Twist it, turn it, hold it up to the sun and moon. Roll it down the byways of your brain and see what sticks to it. Listen to it clank and clunk. Smash it into pumpkin seeds and reassemble it anew. The strength of the slam movement is that it is constantly evolving, rediscovering itself, developing new and effective ways of attracting audience, and making words onstage an enjoyable and profound experience.

Get a picture in your mind of what your ideal slam show would be. A classic competition—no props, no costumes, no musical accompaniment, no performances over three minutes? Would it include dance, aerobics, space shuttles? Would you back it up with a DJ or jazz combo? Score the poets 0 to 50 or rig up some cheesy Applause-O-Meter? How 'bout some farm animals?

Of course, your initial vision is going to get skewed in its execution. That's natural. But if you start with a muddled vision or no vision at all, the show will quickly dissolve into chaos, and spin completely beyond your control.

Ghostboy, the force behind Australia's OutSideRs aRT INc collective combines

poEtrySOUNDscapeshiphopSpoKenWorδ slAminYourFaceOpenMICfreaksPsycho PATHICeXpreSsiOnPERformancePOETRY

into evenings of costume, music, cabaret, wizardry, and pirate games that have electrified the Sunshine Coast with his own imprint of what slam is. What am I talking about? Visit www.outsiders.com.au to experience it for yourself.

Do You Have a Support Network?

Organizing a slam event isn't something you do alone. By its very nature it's communal, a collaboration. You need other people—performers, club owners, bartenders, designers, ticket takers, PR people (to advertise), and an emcee or two. If you have a rich uncle to bankroll your venture, you can hire a staff, but if you're working two jobs just to pay the bills, you're going to be asking favor upon favor.

Does that make you fidget? Well, it should. Collaborating on a shoestring can be frustrating, as frustrating as tying those shoe laces when you're five years old. But it can also be extremely liberating and rewarding, a soul-expanding experience. Slam has drawn writers and poets out of the dreary solitude of their writing-room closets to the joy of creating, performing, and working together collectively.

If you're a control freak and think that you need to do everything yourself to have it done right, one of two things is going to happen; either you'll change or you'll fail. Learning to delegate and rely on other people will free you to focus on more important issues and spare your shoulders some of the burden of being the primary leader. More on this in Chapter 10, "Choosing & Organizing Your Crew."

Do You Have the Time and Energy?

Unreasonable expectations can doom your efforts even before you get started. If you approach the task of organizing a program thinking that you can slap together something on Tuesday for a Wednesday night show, you're going to be sorely disappointed when Wednesday night rolls around. You'll probably begin and end your slam adventure on the first night. Improve your chances of success by going in knowing that the job is tough from the get-go.

Let's add up the time a slammaster will devote to his or her new show over a period of time, say the first six months:

- **Up-front tasks:** Formulating a vision, sketching a show format, scoping out and contracting a venue, lining up talent, READING THIS BOOK, brainstorming the overall promotional campaign, and so on can easily require a minimum investment of ten hours a week for four weeks.

- **Marketing and advertising:** Designing and producing flyers, press releases, and other marketing materials on a regular basis can demand five to ten hours a week, every week. Add another five hours for distribution.

- **Following up:** Calling people, lining up acts, checking your message machine, making sure your performers arrive on time, and writing your newsletter (or updating your website) tacks on another four hours a week, at least.

- **Hiring and training:** Hunting down and hiring door people and sound technicians, interviewing and auditioning hosts and emcees, and replacing staff that quits takes more time and money. Add another five to ten hours, plus a good chunk of aggravation.

- **Running the show:** Plan on starting early in the afternoon. You need to check all those last-minute details. Do you have the markers, scorecards, prizes, and extra chairs? Has someone hung the lights and delivered the sound system? After the show, you'll be lucky if you're packed and ready to head home by midnight. So, let's see, that's four to five shows a month times six months times ten hours per show equals *two hundred and forty hours,* plus or minus a few.

At this point, you might be thinking, "Wait a minute, that's over *eight hundred hours!* More than 130 hours a month. Close to thirty hours a week. Hey, that's more time than I put in at my day job!" It gets easier over time—as your show gets established and gains a rockin' reputation, and you get more people to help you, but in the beginning it's (ugh) real work.

Are You a Show Maker?

You've located a great venue and convinced the owner to let your poets do their thing under her roof. You have some great prospects for open-mic performances. You've lined up some big-name slam poets. You've put together an excellent volunteer staff and spent all week distributing flyers. The chairs are in place, the lights are on, the sound system is perfect, and all the right folks, young and old, are lining up to pay their cover charge. Now what?

YYYYYAAAAAAAAAAAAAAAWWWWWWWWWWWWWNNNNNNNNNNNNNNNNNN

Your show bombs. All those enthusiastic spectators leave bleary-eyed and brain-dead, ready for bed, an apathetic "so so" echoing in their heads. You did everything right, so what happened to make it go so wrong?

Your slam can be well executed technically and still lack the most essential ingredients: flare, spark, drama. The P. T. Barnum, Florenz Ziegfeld, Bill Veeck effect. The nuts and bolts are very important, but the fireworks, the whammy, the zing is what makes people chatter about what rattled their saddles last night.

The lively attractions are what burns your show into the collective memory of your audience and inspires it to advertise your show by word of mouth days after it's over. Don't let your zany creative soul get lost in the business of taking care of business. Show makers are creative animals, risk-takers, fun-builders. And if you don't have a zany, creative side, find someone who does and turn them loose on your plans. Sometimes you need to sacrifice yourself for the good of the show.

Bill Veeck (1914–1986) is a baseball legend and hustler who worked in various capacities for the Chicago Cubs and owned several baseball teams, including the Cleveland Indians, St. Louis Browns, and the Chicago White Sox. He introduced several attractions to liven up the game of baseball, including printing the names of the players on the backs of their uniforms, setting off fireworks after home team home runs, and giving away merchandise to fans.

Are You as Crazy as the Rest of Us?

Starting a slam is like having a kid. Nobody would be insane enough to attempt it if they realized beforehand how much work and heartache were involved. You just need to approach it with a little faith, blind faith. Most of us who started our own slams did it in blissful ignorance—we honestly didn't consider how much sweat and sacrifice it would demand. We were crazy with the itch (I still am). The glorious part of this adventure on which you are about to embark (Hey you've got the itch right?) is that when you get that green gushing monster growing out of the seedling you planted, it spits out fruit in a thousand ways you never, in four millenniums, could have anticipated.

Tallying Your Talents and Resources

People like to talk themselves out of trying new things by convincing themselves that they don't have the knowledge or talent required. In some cases, they're right, but most of the time, these people are just victims of a crisis in confidence. If you've been to a few slam events, dabbled in poetry, created your own greeting cards on a computer, counted money, set the dinner table, or had a productive discussion with a friend, relative, or co-worker, you have at least some of the skills and experiences required to run your own show. You just need to apply those skills in a new way. The following sections help you realize just how much you already know.

Been There, Seen That

You should have attended at least one poetry slam before you even think about creating your own. Better yet, see as many as you can. Skip ahead to Appendix C and find the slam nearest you. Visit it, talk to the slammaster, volunteer to be a judge, and mingle with the slammers. Plan your vacation around slam visits to Texas, Boston, New York, Chicago, the Bay Area—most major metropolitan areas have one or more popular slams. Take a road journal along, jot down impressions, ask advice. You'll be surprised at how much you absorb just by acting like a sponge.

It's one of Slam's principles and an important part of its tradition to readily pass on expertise and experience as a gift to newcomers entering into the slam fold. All of us help each other get started and keep the slam forces flowing and growing.

While you're in the car or on the plane, or throttling your cycle over the Blue Ridge Parkway, think about all the theatrical events you've attended: concerts, plays, puppet shows, bar mitzvahs, holy communions, football games, commencement ceremonies, political rallies, you name it. These are all dramas with rituals you can draw from when creating your slam vision. And if you've been involved with any of these events, even in the smallest capacity, you have valuable practical experience to tap into. Don't discount any of it.

Been There, Done That

At work, at home, at play, wherever you are actively doing something, you're acquiring or sharpening practical skills that you'll use when organizing and running your show. Prior to becoming a full-time poet/performer and slam organizer, I worked as a contractor and gained valuable experience dealing with people on construction sites, battling with architects, and soliciting estimates from subcontractors. All that experience of interacting with fellow humans and dealing with diverse personalities transferred to my work as slammaster and performer. It helped me deal with crotchety club owners, egocentric poets, and headstrong program directors.

If you're married or have a roommate or two, you're picking up valuable negotiating skills. Call on these skills when you need to negotiate with a venue owner or performance poet. If you pay your bills, you have the necessary money-management skills. Apply those skills to make sure your expenses don't outstrip your income. If you've ever designed a cool poster for a science fair, you have a little of what it takes to put together a flyer or a press release. Have you ever hooked up a stereo system or set up a computer? Then you probably have the basic knowledge you need to figure out how to set up and turn on a basic sound system. And if you ever served in a leadership role—as a manager, coach, team leader, or director—you probably have the organizational skills you need to run a slam.

And if you don't ... strap on the seat belt for yet another on-the-job training joy-ride.

Anticipating the Obstacles Ahead

As you know from earlier chapters, slam is not about negativity and discouragement, but before you make the big leap and decide to organize a slam, you should be aware of the inevitable obstacles you will encounter. Oh yes, they're out there—big and small, significant and petty, genuine and political.

If you know what to expect, you'll have a better chance of warding off the blows, tolerating the pain, and recovering when the unavoidable is unavoidable. The following sections reveal some of what goes with the territory.

The Hoity-Toity Establishment

Expect the literary elitists to be jealous and acutely critical. After all, they're protecting their lonely citadels. You have several strategies at your disposal to counteract their attacks: fight them, make fun of them, welcome them into the mix, or ignore them. Pick the most suitable strategy that's akin to your personality. If you're great at debate, go toe to toe. Are you funny? Then poke a joke at them and at yourself to undercut their broadsides. Are you more of a diplomat? Then welcome them into your house and demonstrate your magnanimity as a host. Whatever happens, don't let the establishment change your vision. You can invite the old guard in to be part of your dream, but don't let them remake it. They're yesterday. You're the future.

> Of all the strategies mentioned above, "welcome them to the mix" is the best and often the most rewarding. The naysayers may not join hands at the onset but at least the bridges won't be burned. When your slam's success makes it more opportune for them to cross over, they will.

Most importantly, don't let the sirens of negativity lure you to crash your ship against the rocky shoreline. Slam has no lock on surviving through more than a few generations, but it has proven again and again that it can weather the harshest criticism. Almost every slam has encountered individuals and institutions that actively sought to discredit it, yet nearly all these naysayers have been silenced by the overall success of the slam movement. Plug your ears and sail on. Don't let the cancer of criticism kill a good thing.

Cash Flow Problems

Finances can severely limit the manifestation of your vision. Your wish list may call for a beautiful open stage with top-of-the-line lighting and crystal-clear audio, a glitzy full-color advertising campaign, and top-dollar feature poets. Your wallet, on the other hand, dictates reality: a decent stage that most of the audience can see, a microphone with an amp and a single speaker, black-and-white flyers, and a couple up-and-coming poets who agreed to do you a favor if you'd let them sleep on your couch.

It could get more dismal before it improves. Plan on forking over a chunk of change for advertising, a feature performer, and other expenses without a dime coming back. It's best to set aside a pool of dough to draw on. Money obstacles are always gonna be there. It's the Arts, my friend. But if you have a little nest egg on the side, you'll be better able to ride out the tough times.

Back in 1984, when I started the Get Me High Monday night show, I put $500 out in the first few months without seeing a nickel come back. Seven years later, when Chicago staged the 1991 NPS, pauper poet Marc had $8,000 on the line. Thankfully we sold out the final night championship bout and the money poured in. Costs have escalated. In 1999, Henry Sampson, the NPS tournament director that year, and I each staked $20,000 of our savings in reserve to pay the NPS bills if the event flopped. Of course, it didn't. Whew!

Shifting Sands—Unforeseen Changes

The high profile venue you chose worked out to be the greatest! The shows you envisioned are a perfect match! News has reached your ears that *National Geographic* is going to do a story on your efforts to bring poetry alive in Paw Maw, Indiana...and what?!...the owner's getting divorced?! He's sold the place?! It's closing down next week?! It's going to be converted into Lackluster Video, Inc.?! Oh no!

The unexpected is the worst. It blindsides you. The highway department decides to tear up the street and install a new sewer system outside the front door. They block off the street. The plumbers strike. A two-month project takes almost a year to complete. Someone forgets to put the sidewalk back. In the meantime, the audience shrivels and disappears.

Be ready for the unforeseen obstacles, and have faith that you'll overcome them when they come over you.

Pettiness and Social Hostility

Dealing with the public can be torturous. Prepare for the worst: whining, complaining, attempts to undermine your efforts, back-stabbing, power grabbing, and just about every other negative human characteristic you can imagine. When people are miserable, they take some strange delight in having other people join them. Following is a list of some of the comments you're sure to hear:

"Put me at the top of the open-mic list. I have to leave early."

"Don't put me first."

"I'm reading a poem, why do I have to pay?"

"Why did she get to read three poems, when you only let me read one?"

"I'm sorry to tell you this, but nothing I've heard at your slam is poetry. It's just a bunch of people having group therapy."

"The drinks are too expensive here."

"The food here is pretty bad."

"The judges' scoring was biased toward...republicans...democrats ...feminists...Cubans...race car drivers."

"You think you're quite a big shot don't you."

Be ready to smile, and once in a while politely ask the folks who complain to find someplace else: There's the door. It swings both ways.

If you remember anything, remember...

- You know you have the desire to become a slammaster if you are constantly preoccupied with thoughts of how you would run your ideal show.

- Before becoming a slammaster, be sure you have the necessary resources: a clear vision, a strong and reliable support network, lots of time and energy, the personality of a show maker, and a certain level of insanity.

- You probably have observed enough and done enough to acquire the knowledge and talents required to be an effective slammaster.

- Anticipate problems and keep a little cash on hand for those unexpected expenses and events.

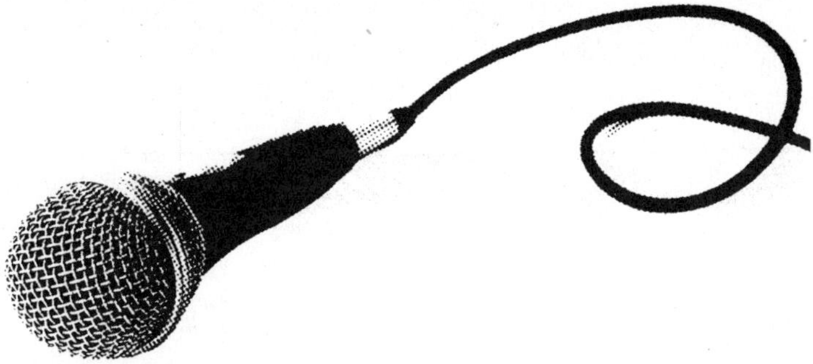

NEXT UP!

5 SHARPENING YOUR VISION

Despite the warnings, obstacles, and your own reservations, you've decided to tear up the turf and tackle your own show. You have the itch, and your inventory indicates that you've got the resources to pull it off.

Congratulations! Welcome to the club. Your next step is to start squinting, angling, and focusing your vision into a pinpoint spot so hot it can blister the kindling and spark a flame. Maybe your mind is cloudy and can't see any form through the fog, or maybe you've already visualized some keen ideas of how to assemble the shards of spectacle floating in your head into a dynamic night of poetry performance.

Time to start welding and polishing that vision to ensure that it's true to your dream and serves your community's needs. You'll have to remain flexible, but you must at least go through the motions of ordering the chaos. If you don't, you're stacking the odds against your dream and in favor of a show that will disappoint you and your audience, and nobody wants that to happen.

This chapter leads you through the soul-searching, vision-focusing process. Use it as a guide, not dogma.

Finding Form in Your Musings

Like any successful *solo* performance, your show must be a unified and entertaining whole, not a discordant hodgepodge of poetry, music, drama, comedy, and whatever else anyone wants to toss into the boil. You're the maestro and conductor, and as such, your job is to orchestrate a pageantry of poetics that plays like a concerto consisting of several movements ... lifting and dropping the audience's emotions, raising its consciousness, and eliciting its most lurid dreams.

To stack up and sort through the possibilities and to guide your good choices, take a closer look at your wants and needs. Consider the questions asked in the following sections, and then ask and answer some of your own.

Look Inside: Identify Your Personal Needs

What do you hope to get out of your slam experience? Do you want an audience for yourself? To create something bigger than a solo performance? To champion forms and styles not recognized by the status quo? To re-create a slam experience you've had elsewhere? To see how far you can push the envelope? To establish a new aesthetic in your community? To provide an opportunity for all the wonderful poets you know? Are you hoping to send a team to nationals and coach them to victory?

Use your answers to adjust your vision. If you're hosting a slam because you want a chance to perform your own poems, work your performance into the show. If you're hoping to recruit members for a slam team, include a fun but official qualifying tournament. If you want to give your poet pals a stage, be sure your show has an opportunity for open-mic performances. And then move on to the next section to tailor your show to your audience.

Look Around: Discover Your Community's Needs

Although it's quite acceptable and common for a slammaster to construct a show without considering the sensibilities of the audience and local poets, it's a little risky. If you don't empathize with the needs of your neighbors, they're probably not going to be very supportive. So ask yourself what you hope your slam will accomplish and how it will serve the community. Will your slam be a platform for young people to express rebellion, for seniors to mix with teens, for minorities to gain a voice, for closet poets to emerge?

Should it be a forum for teaching poetry? A place to go to escape the fashion culture of TV and mass media? A place to have a good time? Do you want to connect and combine all the performing arts into a poetically challenging new form? Do you want your audience to laugh, cry, or be turned upside down, over, and under? All of these? None of these? What does your community need? And how do these factors affect your vision?

Look Back: At What You've Seen & Heard

Sometimes what we and others need and want is revealed in what we've already seen and enjoyed. Think back on all your experiences within the arts, all the entertainment you ingested or participated in. What concerts got your kitchen cookin'? What weekly, monthly, and annual festivals did you mark on your calendar as don't-miss events? What performers and performance styles compel you? What passages of great literature and scenes of great drama were the most moving to you?

By the same token, think about what didn't work. What situations bored the heck out of you? Which poetic styles and postures left listeners drowsy or enraged squirming in theirs chairs ready to dash for the doors or scream "Shut the Fruit Up!"? Which venues had lousy acoustics, poor sight lines, bad air, and sound bleeding through the walls from a polka band or death metal?

From what you have and have not enjoyed you can draw a line to what you desire and what needs to be included in your vision.

Sampling the Many Flavors of Slam

Slams and slam competitions are meant to be liberating creative mixes, doorways opening to new ways of presenting poetry onstage. Readdressing and reformulating the rules and rituals have become almost as important as creating them. The most accepted way of challenging dogmatic slam formulas is to create alternative show formats and competitions. They keep the windows open, minds fresh, the winds of change puffing, and provide rich models for even newer approaches to be conceived.

The following sections describe some of the more interesting slam variations and spin-offs.

The Original Format

The Uptown Poetry Slam, the one that began them all, had three main goals:

1. To provide a formal funky stage for the Chicago Poetry Ensemble, with lighting and a good sound system.

2. To provide a weekly showcase for exploring the concept of a poetry cabaret.

3. Room enough to accommodate the expanding audience for performance poetry.

To satisfy these goals what materialized in my mind (and later manifested itself at the Green Mill) was a two-act show starting with a Get Me High style open mic of eight to ten poets performing one to three poems each. The second act was to feature special guest performers and then move immediately into a theme piece created and performed by the Chicago Poetry Ensemble. I would open and close the show with solo poems.

What evolved out of that vision (and what propelled the show during the first months of its first year) was a three-set format commencing with an open mic that included a couple musical segments, audience plants (poets pretending to be barflies until they broke into verse), and poet ringers (usually members of the CPE) to boost the quality of the open mic. Set two featured one or two guest poets or poetry acts supplemented by a short verse or two by me. And the final set spotlighted CPE but also included a slam competition as a closing tag on a full evening of performance.

The original show retains its cabaret feel to this day, but allowing it to morph and evolve was key to its long-term success.

The Unseen Slam

In the UK, slammers created an event they call the Unseen Slam. It consists of three rounds, or "heats" as they call them over there. The first heat takes place before anybody sits down, while people are still milling about in the lobby or on the street. A hat filled with the first lines of well-known and not-so well-known poems is passed around. Poets who want to jump into the fray, pull out a line, and scribble away for the next half hour creating a new work inspired by the words drawn from the hat.

At the end of that half hour the audience sits down and the show begins. The contestants perform their freshly written treasures onstage, and when all have been heard, the judges present their scores by holding up cards with numbers on them. Low scores get dropped, and the lucky high-scoring scribblers move on to a second heat—another impromptu writing exercise.

This time the audience shouts out suggestions of words that the semi-finalists have to use in a poem they compose over the next fifteen minutes. Once again, at the end of the writing time, the audience listens to the poets present their poems, witnesses the scoring, and consoles those low scoring contestants who get knocked out.

In the final heat, two poets remain onstage, each having to write yet another poem based on random suggestions from the host with the whole audience looking on…in just fifteen minutes! Talk about pressure! The poet who turns out the best poem and best performance (in the eyes of the audience) is declared the winner.

A similar type of impromptu slam occurs in the states inspired by antics at the Green Mill: The Dumb Rhyming Word Game. The audience is asked to shout out three words that the poet contestants must employ in a text they write during the early portion of an open mic. The catch is they must not only use the words but also rhyme them in the context of the poem.

Theme Slams

A *theme slam* is a wonderful way to get poets off the same old topics. How many times does an audience want to hear "war is bad" or "love is good?" A theme slam can catapult slammers to new heights (and sometimes lower depths) challenging and exposing new and old beliefs.

The Ad Man Slam, The Topless Slam, The Dog Walk Slam, and The What Santa Didn't Bring Me for Xmas Slam have inspired some far-out poetic creations.

It's important not to interpret the theme too narrowly. It's meant to inspire, not restrict. So when a poet barely mentions toothpaste in the "Brush Your Teeth Slam," don't disqualify him. On the other hand, if someone performs an experimental verse about modern dance motifs at the "Mother's Day Slam" he might deserve to be booed off the imaginary dance floor.

> [Spoken in a fast conspiratorial semi-whisper, artificially modulated:]
> We're at the Get Me High
> in Chicago, Illinois, tonight!
>
> The audience doesn't know it,
> But I concealed a microphone in myself,
> In an organ Not Even Bleach Can Reach! Let's listen!
> [Loud, fast, and even more artificial than before]

The man of the minute, the 30 second spot!
A man who belieeeeeves leeeeeves in the gorgeous package
    And what's inside!
If I sound excited it's because I AM!
I was born to play this instrument!
And think what it will mean if there are children in the family!
And yet, at the end of purchase time (and provided script),
I can't turn it off.
Phrases of excitement, amazement and pleasure
Are the only sounds I've got to deal with the world!
And it doesn't feel good.
The principal of the school in which my son is not doing well tells me,
"The boy's behavior has got to stop."
I try to sell a mystery ingredient,
"I will take a firmer hand."
At the sound of my voice, the principal recoils,
Recognizing the sound of soap.
–from "Adman" by Ron Gillette

Pong Jam Slam—Music to the Poetic Ear

During the late eighties and all through the nineties into the 21st century many a Sunday night at the Green Mill were reserved for the Pong Jam Slam. Poets were invited to perform to the musical accompaniment of the Pong Unit. At times it was magical. (At times, a train wreck.) The poets asked for any type of music they thought might enhance their text—"super comic hero music," "Russian folk mixed with salsa," "low down muddy water blues"—and the band provided it. If the poet found the groove, a whole new level of experience enriched the night.

The Pong Unit had several configurations. Bass player Steven Hashimoto and guitarist Michael Kent Smith were the primary composers of the music that accompanied my words and the leaders of the jam sessions. Other members included Heath Chappell, Ted Sirota, and Brian Duke on drums, and Carter Luke, Bob Long, and David Flippo on the piano.

This is ancient history. Poetry and musical instrumentation have been partners since Pan tooted his flute and Homer plucked the lyre.

Our most recent poetic ancestors did the same. Carl Sandburg traveled throughout the Midwest reciting poems to the strums of his guitar, usually out of tune. Jack Kerouac's spontaneous style of writing was deeply influenced by the phrasings of bebop.

The world of slam continues this tradition. For years legendary slam champion Cin Salach combined her poems with the music of the Loofah Method and Ten Tongues. Vancouver slammer CR Avery is his own one-poet band, creating complementary rhythms on harmonica and piano to meld with his words. The Jeff Robinson Trio holds musical court with slam poets at the Lizard Lounge in Boston.

Other Slam Spin-Offs—An Ever-Evolving Art

Think of the slam movement as a wild mythological beast that keeps growing and changing. What makes it evolve into some new, wondrous creature? You do. Your vision gives it another eye, another leg, new organs. Sometimes it doesn't look pretty, but it keeps creeping along. Others before you have changed its course, others after you will, too. Here are a few more spin-offs of note:

- **"Chick" Slams:** Girls, girls, girls! Chick slams go by all sorts of pseudonyms from "Estrofest!" to "Labia Poetica," but they all have one thing in common: these slams are for gals only. (This ain't old man Marc being sexist "hssssss"; the women have demanded and spun these off themselves.) All-female poetry nights have gained a great deal of popularity among college-age women, but certainly aren't limited to campus life. Many organizers of all-female poetry events find that these shows garner great work from female poets who feel put off by the often male-dominated, testosterone filled competitive arenas.

- **Improv Slams:** An improvisational theater group in Florida used slam poets to inspire a new improv theater game. One or two slam poets kick out poems that act as a springboard for the improv group to create scenes based on the imagery, cadence, subject matter, and/or the characters found in the poem. Scoring is optional. The game expands the landscape of the poem and interlaces drama and poetry in an exciting new way.

- **Relay Slam:** Another format from the UK is a freestyle event called the "relay" slam. Groups of poets take the stage, and then the audience calls out words. A poet grabs one of those words like it's a jump ball and begins to dribble, creating poetic lines for as long as he can. When he's empty he passes it to another poet. A referee host monitors the event, keeping the action going by prompting the audience to chime in with new words, themes, and ideas until the poets start to sputter. Often music is added to keep a pulse going while the verses are being invented. At the end of the relay, the audience decides by applause who was its favorite Slam Relay Word Dribbler.

- **Drama Slam:** Several theater groups in Chicago and around the world have created drama slams: short scenes presented by competing ensembles judged by thumbs-up/thumbs-down ballots. Thespians use these events as fund-raisers for their next season's subscription series.

- **Music and Dance Slams:** Musicians and tap dancers have put their own twist on the standard slam. Band slams and tap dance slams have brought great joy to audiences. Often, as a nod to the slam community, performance poets are included in these events lacing words through the rhythm of tapping heels and toes.

- **Prop Slam:** As a reaction to the "no prop rule," and to have some outrageous fun, most NPS tournaments include a Prop Slam as a side event to the official proceedings. The most memorable of these can't be described herein for obvious PG reasons. But other spectacles have included wheeling performers in on hospital gurneys to accentuate a poem about sloth, a six-foot submarine sandwich torn apart onstage to emphasize gluttony, and a mesmerizing performance by a man and woman duet using heavy chains and garbage can lids to create a jangling rhythm behind a multivoiced poem about roaming the alleys of Chicago.

- **Cover Slam:** To celebrate all the great poems of the past and present, many slams hold "cover" slams. The rule requiring original work is discarded and performers pay a nod to their favorite poets or poems by performing works that are not their own. The authors they cover can be from centuries ago such as Rumi or Petrarch; or contemporaries such as former poet laureate Billy Collins or Pulitzer Prize winner Mary Oliver. Many times slammers pay tribute to their heroes in the slam community and to each other. The Cover Slam is another way of reminding slammers that slamming is not suppose to be about "I...I...I...I." It's about a "we" that goes back to the dawn of the word.

Heading for the Nationals—Serious Slammin'...Sort of

Every year, slam teams and individual performers from across the United States and even outside the United States gather to perform, compete, network, and party hardy at the PSI-sponsored National Poetry Slam. In 2003, poets representing 60 American cities and three from Canada descended on Chicago. Many more wanted to come.

The National Slam grew to over 80 cities in 2007 and may continue to grow in years to come. Out of necessity, to preserve some semblance of order and prevent it from becoming a logistic nightmare, PSI has instituted a litany of regulations governing who can and cannot compete. Teams and individuals must meet these criteria to be selected and invited to national events.

If your primary intention for starting a slam is to form a team and participate in PSI sponsored events, you need to be aware of the following rules and regulations:

- **Only certified slam teams may compete.** The national tournaments were created to encourage the development of local slams. To support that end, all the teams and individuals competing at national events must come from *certified local slams*—shows that are ongoing and serving a specific community.

- **Each local slam must conduct an open competition to select its team members.** This policy prevents any unscrupulous person from recruiting the top performance poets from around the country and engineering a team of ringers. Don't laugh; it's been done.

- **Individuals may qualify.** In some cases it's possible to compete in national events as an individual. If no regular slam is in your area or if the local slam just started and can't get it together to send a team, you may qualify. And even if you don't get into the official competition, you can participate in the many fringe events at the nationals.

- **Participants must be members of PSI.** Poetry Slam, Inc. (PSI) manages the national tournament and requires that all competitors be members of its nonprofit association. Membership levels range from $15 per year to $1,000 for the big shot donors.

The rules and regulations for PSI events are ever evolving. Go to www.poetryslam.com to get latest eligibility requirements for membership, certification, and national events.

If you remember anything, remember...

- Look inside, around, and back to get a clear vision of what you want your slam to be.

- Slam started as wide open poetic cabaret and continues to morph and evolve; that's what it's meant to do.

- Slam spin-offs abound, and it's okay for every new slammaster to spin out some more.

- If you're going to nationals, get tight with the rules and regulations.

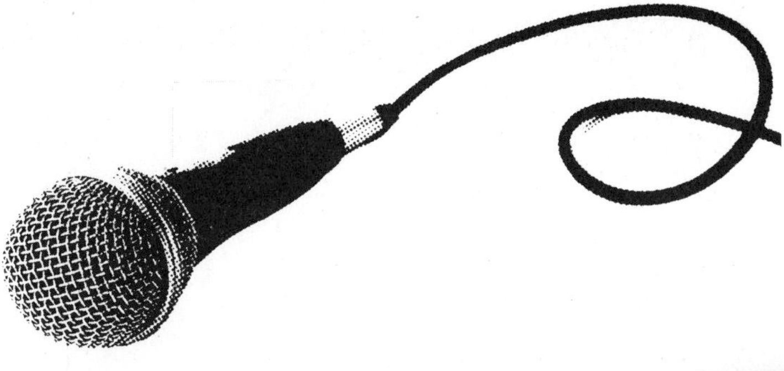

NEXT UP!

The Entertainment Express—Scheduling Departure and Arrival Times

The Main Station Stops

Greetings
Open Mic
Special Acts and Guest Performers
The Competition
Adding Some Bulk to Our Bare Bones Schedule

Detailing Your Trip Tick

Lace the Evening with Ceremony and Ritual
Bring It On—Heckles, Jekylls, and Hydes
Jacks in the Box
To Spin or Not to Spin?
Fleshing Out Our Sample Slam Journey

Final Considerations

Pace

Marketing Power
Leave 'Em Wanting More

If you remember anything, remember...

6 Plotting Your Show: All Aboard Slampapi's Entertainment Express

All slams ultimately take on a life of their own despite what their parents had planned for them, but the best slams always start with a vision and some sort of itinerary. You know when the show starts, who's going to warm up the crowd with an opening act, when the open mic performers will step forward, and how you're going to close out the show. By having a structure in place, you can more effectively lead the audience through an emotional journey of ups and downs that ultimately ends with a bang, not a whimper.

A show's structure is not (or should not be) mechanical. No cookie-cutter format can stamp out sure success in every location. No two slam visions fit comfortably into the same mold. Organizational limitations, the physical nature of the venue, the stage particulars, the lighting and sound capabilities, the seating arrangement, as well as the acts that parade on and off the platform are variables that make every slam unique. The most successful shows evolve organically out of the slammaster's vision, the venue, and the talent she has at her disposal.

As you begin thinking about your slam—your vision, your venue, and the talent you've booked—the form it needs to take might slap you in the face. All you have to do is jot it down. Most of the time, however, you'll need to lay a structure on top of your vision—a schedule that shapes it within the pulsing framework of time. It must pop at the start like a pistol crack, build momentum, and cross the finish line like a steam locomotive. Along the way, it must take the audience on a wheeling joy ride, with peaks and valleys, jumps and curves, sidesplitting surprises, and a conclusion that leaves every heart and mind beaming with transformation.

Climb aboard. In this chapter we're going to build a sample slam excursion. We'll call it Slampapi's Entertainment Express, and we'll build it from the ground up, suspended in time, plugging in the essential stops and hitting them with a whistle, clang, and hoot 'n' hollar.

The Entertainment Express—Scheduling Departure and Arrival Times

When should your show start? When should it end? Talks with the venue owner may have already determined this. She may have made it clear that her full wait staff does not come in until 7:00 p.m. and that they need a good hour to set up before they can handle heavy crowds. Your slam can't start before 8:00 p.m. and it can't run later than midnight, because that's when Lurch bolts the doors shut. Do you want to be slammin' till the clock strikes midnight? It's your choice, but I suggest that you tune the length of your show to an established entertainment model. (Skip ahead to Chapter 7 for tips on what days and times to stage your show.) Here are some examples:

- **Theater productions:** One-act plays with no intermission run from one to one and a half hours. The common time frame for a two-act play with a fifteen-minute intermission is two hours, plus or minus a few minutes. On occasion a play will run three hours or more with two or three intermissions, but it had better be outstanding.

- **Nightclub acts:** Club time is divided into sets, not acts. The duration of sets varies from a brief thirty minutes to a very long one-hour-and-forty-minute set. Between sets are intermissions that range from ten to twenty minutes. A three-hour show consisting of three forty-minute sets and two twenty-minute intermissions is standard, and it goes up and down from there. It's very rare for people to come out for an evening of only one forty-minute set, and if they do, they can easily feel cheated if that forty minutes doesn't contain something extraordinary.

- **Festivals:** Festivals customarily have many activities operating simultaneously throughout the day and night. They seldom begin their schedules before 11 a.m. and usually wrap things up by 10 or 11 p.m. Activities are commonly divided into forty- to fifty-minute chunks and are sometimes staggered so that folks can attend as many sessions as humanly possible. If your slam is the showcase act of a festival, it might be allowed a double or triple time slot at a prime hour, affording it the opportunity to attract the most attention and the largest audience. If you're one of the side shows, you could be stuck anywhere in the schedule. Be sure your show concept fits with the time slot it's assigned.

- **Cultural arts events:** Programming for community arts events sponsored by cultural organizations can take place any time during the day to correspond to the types of audiences the programmers are trying to attract and serve. Noontime concerts for the lunch crowd, morning book circles for seniors, after-school workshops for students, and nighttime hullabaloos for the community at large are just a sampling of available possibilities. In general, cultural arts events are family friendly, start early, and never linger too late into the evening.

Although your vision along with your departure and destination points drive the train, don't be afraid to switch tracks, shift cars, pull back on the throttle, or jam it to the floor. Remember, your slam is an adventure rigged with intriguing detours along the way. As its conductor, you'll need to draw up an itinerary—a schedule of starts and stops and switches. As conductor and tour director, you'll need to choose which site and stations to accent or expound upon and which ones to abbreviate.

For our sample slam show itinerary, let's say that the action will make its first chug forward at 9:00 p.m. on Tuesday night, and it *will* run until the clock strikes midnight. We're going to design it to hold two and a half hours of antics, reserving a half hour for late arrivals and run-over time. The owner has asked us to include two fifteen-minute intermissions for selling drinks to keep the servers grateful and subdued during performances, especially if the performers and patrons tip well.

Slampapi's Entertainment Express	
8:00	Doors Open, load-in, and setup
9:00	Opening Set
9:45	—break—
10:00	Set Two
10:45	—break—
11:00	Final set
11:50	Closing ritual

Every slam has a beginning, middle, and end.

The Main Station Stops

Now that we know how much travel time we have, the next step in creating our slam itinerary is to mark on our route the types of sites we want our travelers to visit. In drama, we call these sites *plot points*—episodes where the action takes a turn, a flip, or a spin and arrives at a new perspective that acts as the next departure point. The following sections describe the most familiar, rock-solid station stops on any slam journey.

Greetings

Memorable slam experiences begin as soon as someone walks through the door. How slammasters, hosts, volunteers, and emcees meet, greet, and treat people as they enter and occupy the venue influences people-to-people interaction throughout the night. If folks are shy or made to feel isolated when they enter, they're likely to be reserved or aloof, making even the liveliest of shows a dreary affair. Before things get popping onstage, seize the opportunity to set the mood with some ceremony and ritual:

- **Introduce strangers to one another.** Make a game of it. Appoint an audience member as each week's meet-and-greet-person or have your assistant handle the greetings. Tell folks it's part of the game...which it is.

- **Begin your event with preshow music or antics.** Playfully taunt and dare poets (and non-poets) to sign up for the open-mic set. Initiate informal table-to-table create-a-stanza sessions. Pass around a photo album displaying virgin virgins **from** prior events. Have a table shout out a favorite line from a classic poem across the room challenging another table to shout back their own favorite line. Any activity that stirs people to life and breaks the icicles off their ears and eyes will do.

- **Open your show with a bang.** Stage a grand entrance of performers, a parade through the venue. Add a little emcee spiel. Initiate the virgin virgins who signed up for the open mic by baptizing them with a spray can labeled Bad Verse Repellant, or surprise everyone with a spontaneous, in-audience ensemble round robin ending with the emcee center stage behind the microphone shouting, "Are We Ready to Slam?!?"

Round robin is a term we used in Chicago to describe a series of very short poems performed one right after another by several poets planted at different locations in the audience. The trick was to jump in right on the heels of the preceding poet's last line and hold back the audience's response until all the poems had been delivered. Round robins build to a palpable tension and burst into a crowd roar on the final syllable.

Open Mic

Stick your open-mic session at the beginning of your show and keep it relatively brief—eight to ten poets performing one or two poems each. The open-mic session provides a good warm-up for the features who follow, gives aspiring slammers an opportunity to perform, equips the emcee with a gauge of where the audience's mood is hovering, and provides a buffer zone for late arrivals. And if by chance one of your open micers rocks the house with a stellar performance, so much the better; the baseline has been set from which you can launch the rest of the show challenging what follows to equal or exceed your opening act.

Placing the open mic at the beginning of the night was key to the success of the Uptown Poetry Slam. It went against entrenched thinking that the open mic "amateurs" should be dumped at the end of a very long evening of "accomplished" poets. The outcome of that bad thinking was a fidgeting audience of wanna-be readers fumbling through their folders concerned more about their upcoming turn onstage than the words uttered by the special guest. That collective impatience was at times so overwhelming that even a short powerfully presented set by the guest poet seemed interminable.

To quiet the grumblings and retain control over the number of open mic participants, draw names out of a fish bowl or hat to determine who goes onstage and when. Always reserve space for virgin virgins and newcomers, but stick the names of those who've been to your show a few too many times into the bowl or hat and let fate (and your cunning handiwork) determine who speaks and who doesn't.

Take liberties with the order. If the open mic has become a pain-inducing funeral march and you know that Josie's got a steamy poem that will end the torture, get Josie onstage immediately, whether she's six names down the list or last. Pull names out the fishbowl that aren't even in the fishbowl. Your job is to create a good show and entertain the audience, not to be a slave to poet etiquette and protocol.

As a slammaster, you will without a doubt encounter *repeat offenders,* open-mic cronies who travel from show to show and bore audiences with the same laborious poems and styles they've been regurgitating for years. If you're too generous with them, they'll come back week after week, overstaying their welcome and killing the excitement and spirit of your show. Don't let them do it. Put their names at the bottom of the list and bear no guilt if you forget to call them, "Oh I'm sorry Bob, not enough time tonight." You might think this unjust, even cruel (maybe it is), but I guarantee you'll be eager to adopt this harsh policy after you've listened to "Bob" read the same blessed poem seven weeks in a row.

Special Acts and Guest Performers

Headliners draw crowds. Nobody eagerly climbs aboard a tour bus to view the ever-unchanging landscape of the flatlands. Your slam excursion has to include guaranteed crowd-pleasin' sites to visit, experience, and treasure—proven specialty acts and performers who'll rock the rafters. It's your job to place them at strategic points along the track's path to raise the stakes and create the scenic and sometimes breathtaking peaks. Select acts that offer a new flavor, sound, or visual component contrasting or complementing what precedes them.

I've found that a fifteen- to twenty-minute set for guest performers is optimum. I usually ask them to have a couple encores ready in case the crowd screams for more. I've witnessed a few great performers hold the stage for forty minutes and still leave the crowd wanting more, but only a few.

The guest spots are where you can experiment with different styles of spoken word entertainment. It can be risky, but if you've scouted and seen something wild and word wonderful succeed on another stage, or if you've received good reports about this mad new form of rap-sonnet from a half dozen slammasters, give it a go on your stage to see if it clicks or clunks.

The Competition

For most slams, the competition is the show within the show—the whip cream topping on a fancy dessert. Everything leading up to it—the emcee chatter, the open micers, the specialty acts and guest performers—may have filled the bellies to an almost peak satisfaction, but there's always room for dessert. The competition is the dance festival regaling in the plaza at the end of the tour, the jousting match on the queen's lawn, the duel duked out on a foggy wharf while the sailors and writers and lovers huddled in the tavern doorway watch with glimmering eyes. It has its own specific structure, suspense, conflict, and characters, a classic drama:

- Beginning with the emcee spiel, the introduction of judges and naming of contestants, the announcement of the prizes, and the explanation of the rules. And then proceeding to the...

- Middle consisting of preliminary bouts and rounds, coin tosses, poets jumping on and off the stage, score cards held high in the air, booing, cheering, personality traits exposed and magnified, performers spouting and pouting, emcee's ushering sore losers off and adding emphasis to potential champions, the crowd's reactions, and the poems themselves, leading to the climatic...

- End encompassed in the final round, the playoff between the best competitors, the audience's bias informed by the earlier rounds, the suspense leading to the final scoring, the announcement of the winner, and the awarding of the prize.

Placing the competition at the end of your show gives the night a natural climax, a clear target and closing. By contrast, starting your show with the full competition (its beginning, middle, and end) can make everything that follows feel anti-climatic. Dividing the competition into segments spread throughout the evening squeezed in between other acts can be an okay choice, but sometimes it disrupts the unity and cohesiveness of the evening, especially if patrons are coming and going.

Adding Some Bulk to Our Bare Bones Schedule

The slam competition is our final destination—our show's climax and denouement—so we'll devote the major portion of our itinerary to it. We'll limit the open-mic session to weed out the windbags and provide stage time for newcomers who really have something fresh to say. We've recruited a local singer/songwriter to play blues instrumentals for fifteen minutes during the preshow segment as the host signs up poets and greets people. Our itinerary is beginning to mature.

Slampapi's Entertainment Express

8:00	Doors Open, load-in, and setup
8:30	Host greets and seats the audience performing impromptu haikus at several tables based on the names of the people she's seating
8:45	Guy Blue performs preshow instrumentals and finishes his set with a sing-along
9:00	Emcee/host welcomes everyone and performs high-energy poem/song duet with Guy Blue
9:05	Emcee spiel advising the audience about what's to come and how they can participate
9:10	Open mic poets drawn from fish bowl
9:20	Virgin virgin poets
9:40	Closing poem with band incorporating a three poet round robin into the mix
9:45	—break—
10:00	Guest performer #1
10:20	Guest performer # 2
10:40	—break—
10:55	Guy Blue plays high-energy tune to open set
11:00	Slam rituals and emcee spiel
11:05	Introduction of judges
11:10	Ritualize explanation of the rules

11:15	Slam competition
11:50	Awarding prize to the winner
11:55	Closing poem and good-byes

Our slam begins to take some interesting turns.

Detailing Your Trip Tick

So far we've been viewing our slam excursion trip from a balloon floating above the hills and vales, zoomed out to get a general idea of the overall landscape. Now we're gonna swoop down for a more intimate incursion—to sample the special flavors, customs, and surprises that can elevate your show from mediocre to magnificent. As we proceed, jot down any twists and turns that come to mind, any special detours or roadside attractions you might add to further heighten the adventure. You're the tour guide, it's your artistic vision, so grab anything and everything that has the potential to further your vision.

Lace the Evening with Ceremony and Ritual

All planned human events have ceremony and ritual. At birthday parties we turn out the lights, bring in the cake aglow with burning candles, and sing off-key. At sporting events we stand and choir the national anthem, toss a coin, face-off, or shout "Play ball!" Ceremony and ritual frame an event, giving the audience familiar guideposts that get them involved and pique and fulfill their expectations. The more imaginative you are when creating ritual and ceremony, the more hooked your audience will become.

We've already touched upon and described many slam rituals: treating newcomers as virgin virgins; the snapping, stomping, and groaning of disapproval; greeting people at the door when they arrive; selecting and introducing judges; and drawing names out of a fish bowl. Here are a few more examples of rituals used at various slams around the world:

- **House Rules.** Almost every long-running slam has developed certain house rules that the emcee explains at the beginning of the show. "All heckles must be more intelligent than the poem heckled." "If a poet dedicates a poem to someone in the audience, that person must come onstage during the performance of the poem." The spiel gets repeated every week and provides a blueprint for performers and the audience, advising them on how they should behave and what they can expect.

- **Initiating the New.** Many slams have a ceremony to shine a spotlight on first-time audience members and poets. They could all be brought to the stage to compose an *exquisite corpse* or just be asked to stand and name their favorite poet. This all must be done in a fun-loving spirit without rigidly enforced participation. Acknowledging and identifying newcomers helps fold them into the tribe and usually doesn't require any bloodletting...usually, anyway.

An *exquisite corpse* is a poem that many poets (often everyone in the room) construct by adding a line to a preceding line, usually having seen or heard only the preceding line.

- **Counting Out the Dollars.** Slams that pay cash prizes sometimes have the emcee and audience count out the prize money dollar by dollar. Some slams provide several prizes from which to choose, and the audience watches with interest to see whether the winning poet chooses the red bikini underpants or the "I'm a Poet, Too!" T-shirt.

- **Shout Out.** A few slams have community poems they recite en masse each week, sort of like a church hymn or the national anthem, which express the commonality and purpose of everyone there.

The ritual and ceremony you pack into your slam provides an underpinning of structure and entertainment that can save it from disaster should your guest performers and/or slam competitors bomb. The booing ritual has saved many a home team loss from becoming a total waste of an afternoon at the ballpark.

When developing rituals, consider your audience. What will they find fun and engaging? Should the audience members tap their feet when a performance starts to fade? Should the emcee ask an audience member to choose the next open-mic performer? Should performers call out challenges to one another? Should the judges be brought onstage to explain their scoring?

Bring It On—Heckles, Jekylls, and Hydes

Many poetry circles and slams (too many in my opinion) discourage hecklers and any negative reactions from the audience. Others not only allow it, but make a special point of informing the audience that they have permission to voice their opinions, positive or negative. Aggressive audience participation is a foundation of the slam. It's what set slam apart from the failing traditional readings of the late '70s and early '80s. It created an atmosphere of honest feedback that forced the early slammers to develop better performance skills and more accessible texts. Of course, it's your show, and the choice is yours, but I strongly encourage you to at least consider giving patrons the license to express their displeasure over a poem or performance that insults or abuses the people who paid to sit in the seats.

Jacks in the Box

A tedious drive across the unchanging flatlands of middle America can be the adventure of a lifetime if you bump into colorful characters along the way or know that your sexy sweetheart is awaiting your arrival.

Likewise, your slam should provide some unexpected pleasures, some titillating surprises, and enough roadside attractions to accent the landscape along the way.

As slammaster, you must build suspense—inflate expectations for the upcoming performances without lifting the curtain too high and revealing too much. If you cultivate no expectations, if the audience doesn't think that there's something ahead worth waiting for, they're going to bolt at the first dull performance.

Here are a few suggestions for building suspense at your slam:

- Introduce the competing slammers as longtime rivals facing off for blood and honor. Add a few dollars to the prize pot and pass the hat around, prodding the audience to kick in a few bucks to sweeten the pot and heighten the stakes for the grudge match.

- Initiate impromptu collaborations between guest performers and audience members. For instance, if your friend Barry the Blues Harmonica is in the audience, instruct Emcee Joan Anne to pull him up onstage to perform a duet with HeAmHe, your guest performer from New Jersey. Audiences love spontaneous collaborations, even when they crash and burn.

- Have your in-house ensemble stage an argument (about poetry of course) that breaks into a verse dialogue across the bar.

- Jump up onto the bar and kick out a poem while dancing between drinks. Shut out all the lights and have everyone whisper a poem into the ear of the person next to them.

To Spin or Not to Spin?

Onstage DJs behind a couple turntables spinning and scratching tunes before, after, and during slams are now a common sight and sound, especially at shows that cater to the younger crowds. Done with style and the sense of the diversity that slams seek to encourage, tossing some music into the mix with the help of a designated DJ can add an exciting background to an evening. However, in the wrong hands, spinning can burden your show with tedium and alienate many wavelengths of the broad slam audience spectrum. A DJ who spins a narrow selection of beats, engineers the music to be more important than the words, or inspires each and every poet to be a rapper might be better suited for a Hip Hop showcase. On the flip side, if your show is a bit sleepy and you can't afford to hire live musicians, a DJ might be just the needle you need to scratch the groove.

Fleshing Out Our Sample Slam Journey

To boost attendance we lined up a local literary hero to make a cameo appearance, and our in-house ensemble is ready to try out some new material. So let's work those elements and a few more into our itinerary.

Our slam in its full glory.

Slampapi's Entertainment Express

8:00	Doors open, load-in, and setup
8:30	Host greets and seats the audience performing impromptu haikus at several tables based on the names of people she's seating
8:40	Guy Blue performs preshow instrumentals and finished his set with a sing-along.
9:00	Emcee/host starts her ritualized welcome and is interrupted by the in-house ensemble performing a round robin that leads into a high- energy poem/song duet with Guy Blue

9:05	Emcee finishes her welcome and presents the ritualized spiel advising the audience about what's to come and how they can participate
9:10	Open mic poets drawn from fish bowl
9:20	Virgin virgin poets are introduced and interviewed by the emcee while the in-house ensemble creates impromptu poems about the virgins to be presented at close of set
9:40	Closing poem with band incorporating another round robin into the mix for a big finish presenting and focusing on the impromptu poems created about the virgin virgins
9:45	—break—
10:00	Award winning local poet
10:20	In-house ensemble performs new piece
10:40	—break—
10:55	Guy Blue conducts a slam sing-along to open and set the stage for the slam competition
11:00	Emcee spiel and introduction of judges during which the emcee requires each of the judges to perform some stunt with the in-house ensemble to prove that they're qualified
11:10	Explanation of the rules
11:15	Round One: five poets read one poem each—the two low scores are dropped
11:30	Round Two: three poets read one poem each—the low score is dropped
11:40	Round Three: the two remaining poets read one poem each and the winner is awarded the prize
11:50	Emcee calls Big John the doorman to come to the stage and count out the cash prize dollar by dollar to the winner
11:55	Emcee closes out the show with a short poem followed by a closing instrumental by Guy Blue

Final Considerations

Now look over your planned itinerary. Check it against the notes you jotted while reading earlier chapters about the style and vision. Be sure all your plans are compatible with your venue setup and technical capabilities. Does your itinerary balance with your budget? Are there highly marketable features to it? All yesses. Okay you're almost there. Just a few more things to consider.

Pace

A good show keeps rolling forward under its own momentum, pinching the audience's attention as it proceeds. This seemingly "natural" momentum is usually due to the creative elements you've sown into it, the maneuverings of a competent emcee, and a surprise or two that re-captivates the audience. And the pacing of all of it has to be right. Your show should move forward and upward as a series of crescendos that rise and plateau, rise and plateau, each time to a higher level. The peaks should rise to an ultimate climax very close to the last syllable of the show.

If you were to draw a graph of a finely constructed show, it would look like a mountain range rising from foothills to midsize mountains to high sierras to snowcaps to Mt Everest to a lover's leap drop-off at the end, with folks floating on clouds gently down to sea level as they put on their coats to leave. When structuring your show, make it Bing-Bang-Boom interesting out of the starting blocks, but make sure it crosses the finish line with a BLAST!!! that rumbles and roars.

Marketing Power

If your show plan does contain a bing-bang-boom format, you should have no problem finding aspects of your lineup to highlight in your marketing and promotional campaigns. If you can't seem to find anything to legitimately praise in your flyers and press releases, take another look at the roster. Have you included any well-known, well-loved poets in the evening's festivities? Have you created or borrowed some fascinating style of judging the competition? Is rewarding all virgin virgins who dare to take the stage with a copy of *The Outsiders Bible of Verse* something you can promote in your neighborhood?

Anything unique can add marketing power to your advertisements and holds potential for attracting audience. If your show doesn't have any headline grabbers, you'd better find something to boost its promotional appeal.

Leave 'Em Wanting More

Touch them and they'll stick with you through the mediocrity. Overburden them, even with great stuff, and they'll stay away for years. All audiences have a saturation point, so end your show before it reaches that point. An astute emcee can sense when the "that's enough" line approaches. If you, as the host or emcee, are unsure of whether the audience wants more or not, just ask them, "Have you had enough yet?" They might be polite and say "No" when they really mean "Yes," but if the screams for more are sincere, you've got clear approval to slam on. If not, wrap it up. Sometimes, a little less really is more.

If you remember anything, remember...

- Establish an overall structure for your show to give it form and direction.

- Your show should be engaging from start to finish, rising in intensity and quality as the evening progresses.

- Focus on the fundamentals of your show: the emcee, the open-mic performers, the feature artists, the in-house ensemble, and the ever-unpredictable audience.

- Use the slam competition near the end of your show to ramp up expectation and energy. Decide on a system of scoring that engages and entertains the audience.

- Don't feed your audience any more than they can swallow. Your show should exceed their expectations, but leave them hungry for more.

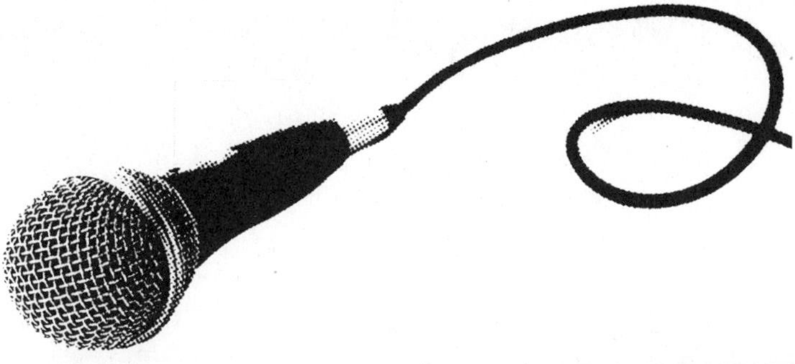

NEXT UP!

Compose a Venue Wish List

Size Matters

Think Small—Small Enough to Create a Happening

Think Bigger...When Necessary

Going Colossal

Ambience Is Everything

Designed for Comfort

Dripping with Character

Supportive Service Staff

Enthusiastic Clientele

Conducive Background Music

Consistency

A Supportive Owner

Frame the Picture

What About the Stage?

Checking for Essentials: Necessary Services

7 SCOPING OUT THE RIGHT VENUE

Now that you've got a crystallized concept of your show crawling in your head, it's time to find a playhouse for that brainchild of yours—a suitable spot for poets to perform and patrons to kick back. It can be anything from a neighborhood dive to the basement of the public library. It can blare bold neon or hunker down under a dimly lit street lamp. It can have the java-juiced ambience of a coffeehouse or the shake, rattle, and roll of a dance club.

Whatever your target venue is, it must be the right size, shape, and location to attract a crowd and have the potential to cultivate the desired personality your brainchild is crying for. But what's the right size and shape? What's the right crowd? How do you select a venue that provides your show with the best chance to succeed? This chapter answers all these questions and more as it coaches you on how to scope out the best slam poetry venue in your hood.

Compose a Venue Wish List

The fact that you enjoy hanging out at the Jumpin' Java Bean and the manager's cute does not qualify the place as a top-choice slam venue. It might accommodate only a couple dozen patrons, provide no stage area, or have the look and feel of a dentist office. You might like the joint, but maybe your slam would play better elsewhere.

Always keep in mind that this is business, show business, but business nevertheless, and you want your business to succeed. So shove your personal preferences off to the side and start thinking of your slam show objectively.

> If you've never staged a show, it's okay to make educated guesses. You'll learn more and more as you go along. It's like the process of writing itself. First a blank sheet, then a few scattered thoughts, then more thoughts, and soon a main character, a climax, and a target appear. It all starts to come together and make sense. You can sniff and taste what you're looking for. The choice becomes intuitive. It just happens. You realize, "This is it! This is the place!"

Grabbin' the proper perspective? Good. Now, get ready to scribble a list of criteria to help you spot potential venues. Pretend you're shopping for a new set of wheels. Hardtop or convertible? Manual or automatic? Sedan or sports car? A new honey or one that's shed a little rubber? Each specific narrows the choices and reduces the time and energy you'll spend searching.

Size Matters

Slams shows have played to audiences ranging in size from a handful of squawking bookworms in the hindquarters of a rundown bookstore to thousands of screaming spoken word zealots crowded into a downtown auditorium. It's important to fit audience potential to venue capacity.

Think Small—Small Enough to Create a Happening

If this is your first time at it, think small. Your aim is to create a happening, and happenings spill out the door onto the street. People drive by and see lines of anxious fans pushing to get in. "Hey something's happening in there! Let's check it out." Inside, folks stand shoulder to shoulder, and when they applaud, the roar gets physical. "Hear that? I told you. A happening, man!"

If a club's too big, it sucks the energy out of the event, leaving a hollow shell. The cheers in a half-empty club (even if it has 300 fans scattered through an eight hundred–seat auditorium) echo like whispers in a mausoleum. Harry Houdini could be swimming back from the dead, popping out of his upright watertight glass tank like a spooky fish, and folks would probably say, "Oh, that's nice."

For a newborn weekly slam in a midsize city with some sort of existing literary arts scene (either at the library or at the local book club), anticipate drawing thirty to fifty people, but don't be surprised if eighty or one hundred show up. That's not unusual in the slam world. The venue you choose should feel comfortably occupied with thirty people and like a spilling-out-the-door-call-911 HAPPENING MAN! with one hundred.

Think Bigger...When Necessary

You're moving on up. Your first venue is splitting at the seams. Thinking small isn't what you had in mind. Get a grip. The same principles apply. Estimate your potential audience by adding 10 or 20 percent to your current draw. No matter how successful your present show is, it's probably a mistake to book a "moving-on-up venue" that's double the size of your old one. Starting a spin-off slam isn't a guaranteed success.

Be that as it may, if you're thinking big, consider the following options:

- **Taverns:** Many taverns have a back room with a bandstand that can accommodate crowds of 100 to 150 people or more.

- **Storefront theaters:** Storefront theaters are often available for special events on dark nights between dramatic productions.

- **Auditoriums or event rooms:** Libraries and cultural centers usually have auditoriums and event rooms with seating capacity that may be just right for your moving-on-up ambitions.

If you can hold on to your starter venue while trying out the newer, bigger model, do so. Remember, there are no absolutes in this business. What's gold in one corner of the city could be garbage in another.

Going Colossal

Of course, as a slam community grows larger and larger so do the opportunities for special events of a spectacular magnitude. When that time comes don't limit yourself and the seats you might be able to fill.

One-time events and annual productions bank on huge turnouts to pay the expenses and make the planning efforts worthwhile. Assess your audience potential by surveys, mailing lists, attendance records of past performances, and gauging how many citizens your marketing campaign will reach. Then find the spot that can accommodate your numbers with a little room to spare.

Large auditoriums, concert halls, dance clubs, and theaters have seating capacities ranging from five hundred seats to a few thousand. Final nights of most PSI slam tournaments are usually staged in spaces capable of accommodating a couple thousand people. To date no local slam committee has pumped the mics up in a football stadium, but who knows—maybe one day the Super Bowl halftime show will be a slammin' affair.

Ambience Is Everything

It's the final round of Bout 3 at the Could-Be-You National Slam. Boston vs. LA vs. the dark horse Omaha. Michael Brown, famous slam elder and renowned group-piece strategist, needs the Boston team to score a near perfect 30 to win and move on to the semi-finals. The team is outside having a communal-hug and psyche-up session when the emcee announces, "Next to microphone, Boston! With a group piece!"

Whaawhoo! They squeeze through the kitchen and enter from behind the coffee counter. One team member gets stuck behind the manager, who's sick of this poetry stuff and won't budge. Boston finally takes the stage and starts executing its seductively searing group piece.

And then, the espresso machine blasts out its steam and grind. The manager chuckles. This happened twice before during the first two bouts. The performers recover and recapture the audience's attention. They're halfway through the piece, building momentum, walking the razor's edge, lifting the audience to new heights.

Then...bam! Like the bong of a gong, a frenetic wedding party bunches in through a doorway next to the stage cackling in their insular oblivion. The procession halts, stunned in front of the team's animated choreography, poets emoting in their faces. "Good heavens! What kind of café is this?" They scurry to the counter and titter nervously over a round of lattes.

"The Photographer"
A Speak'Easy ensemble piece written by Robbie Q
(Group punctuates words with camera flashbulbs. Robbie Q has a professional camera.)
Group: Pop Snap Click Kaboom
Pop Snap Click Kaboom
R: Hello, Supermodel
Welcome to my office
You wanna make some real art?
(Molly jumps in to play the supermodel role followed by Tim competing for the attention of the photographer and camera. Robbie divides his attention between the two, playing one against the other.)
Group: Pop Snap Click Kaboom
Pop Snap Click Kaboom
R: I am the hulking invisible
sweating from moment to moment

memory to memory
nimble picture sucking
hands, eyes dancing.
I am your path to immortality...

Though this story is fiction, stuff like this happens all the time. Each year during the planning of the national slam, grumbling resurfaces about the cramped coffee shop with the noisy counter people, gurgling espresso machine, and the manager who insisted on running the grinder in the middle of each and every performance.

Ambience can enhance or diminish a slam's potential. The reading room of the district library or the conference room of the corporate center is not going to infuse the audience with a raucous Elizabethan feel. If you're expecting your crowd to be under-thirty American hardcore rockers, a straight ahead jazz joint ain't gonna spike it, either.

A friendly funky place fits most slams. Slick shiny Las Vegas styled nightclubs have worked, too (though less often). Most successful slam venues share some common traits, "specifics" that create a winning ambience. In the following sections, I describe the most important of these.

Designed for Comfort

A slam venue needs to be a place where people like to hang out whether something's happening onstage or not. A sit-down place with comfortable chairs, stools, and/or couches. Good sight lines to catch the action without leaning or moving or missing something. A place that feels down home.

It's easy to spot this trait. The venue that has it is occupied at all hours of the day by all sorts of people. Once you walk in and sit down, you'll probably stay for a second and third and fourth mug of coffee, tea, or beer. You'll find yourself buying dinner or engaging in a conversation with people you never met before

On the flip side of the tea bag, a venue can be *too* comfortable. If its ambience induces the clientele to *just* hang or chill in a too-cool pose oblivious to performers and performances, regarding them as an animated form of background music, then nix the place. An army of your most devoted fans would be hard-pressed to overcome the ambience of ambivalence.

Dripping with Character

The ideal venue has personality—oddball stuff on the walls, offbeat art, a cheesy theme. Something! Butchie, the owner of the Get Me High Jazz Club, nailed old 45s to the walls and turned the ceiling into a chalkboard for everyone to scribble on. The Green Mill has the rep and feel of a prohibition jazz joint where Al Capone and Machine Gun Jack McGurn hung out and broke noses.

A few slammasters have tried "brand name" venues—franchise bookstores and coffeehouses, and restaurants with facades and logos duplicated from town to town, but not many have survived. Homegrown. Unique. Ma and Pa. Stimulating and authentic does better. It can score 10s all around. Find a venue with a character that fits your vision's plot.

Supportive Service Staff

The servers (sometimes characters themselves) have to be on your team. They can't be taking orders and talking louder than the performers onstage. They can't be flinging empties into the bottle shoot and banging the cash register every ten seconds.

On slow nights Judy, the bartender at the Get Me High, used to lead us all in a limerick circle, each of us rhyming out as many as we could, until the audience finally poured in and the real show (late as usual) got yelping. Gingi, long time waitress at the Green Mill, sang a cappella in between orders during the open mic, scoring some extra tips from an appreciative audience.

Having the *help* behind you can make or break a show.

A mural adds character and soul to the Green Mill.

Enthusiastic Clientele

The regulars are like globs of living color splashed on the walls of a venue's atmosphere. They set the tone. What they do and how they react can give your show an immediate boost or snuff it out like a wet cigarette. If they came to watch the wet T-shirt contest or Monday Night Football, the regulars might treat you and your poetry troupe as a nuisance, in which case your show is doomed before you even step onstage.

Conducive Background Music

Having the right musical accompaniment is a concern mostly in nightclubs, coffee shops, and spots that have a regular day and night business serving the public. The style of ambient music they play through the house sound system or off the jukebox has to be in tune with your vision. "Where Have All the Flowers Gone," for instance, is not going to break well with the hip-hop crowd. Drum & bass may repel the over-forties. Sometimes the owner and management are more than happy to set the tone you want, but sometimes not. On your criteria list, jot down the kind of preshow and intermittent music you desire.

Consistency

A place can have character, but if that character changes from month to month, it's going to create problems. Part of the slam experience is ritual. People come because they know what to expect. They expect the unexpected to happen, but they have faith that the trappings will be familiar. Nothing is more disheartening than arriving at a venue on show night to find the stage has been removed or that they've doubled the price of mixed drinks or that the manager has been replaced for the sixth time and the new one knows nothing about your slam. Keep the surprises onstage and all else on a steady keel.

A Supportive Owner

I've been very lucky; for nearly two decades I've worked with and for one of the finest, most honorable, and supportive owners a show maker could hope for—Dave Jemilo, owner of the Green Mill. He's been an ally, friend, and consultant all these years, and a major factor in the success of my show and other acts that got their start in Uptown.

If your personality clashes with the owner's, hightail it out of there; it's not worth the aggravation.

Talk to the local musicians who gig around your town. They'll fill you in on which club owners, managers, presenters, and curators of entertainment have a clue and which ones don't. The lousy ones are usually new to the biz. You can't have long-term success in the entertainment industry unless you're savvy and personable.

Plan on having several conversations with the owner or main person in charge. They're very busy people and have defense mechanisms for putting off first encounters, so don't expect them to welcome you with open arms. These folks deal with a hundred personalities a day. Get through their defense mechanisms before making an assessment. If your vision clicks with their personality, bingo! You've got a shot at the gold.

Frame the Picture

Visualize the physical action and movement of your show as if you're choreographing a theatrical performance. What will you need for it? A big stage or just floor space? Are there lots of people performing at once? Musicians? Dancers? Do you see light cues changing the mood? A grand entrance of performers on roller skates throwing confetti?

Match that vision to a type of space that could accommodate it. Maybe draw an imaginary floor plan for it, or list its specifics in your criteria notebook, or both. How will your performers maneuver through it? Where will the audience sit?

A venue can have great ambience, but if performers are bumping into columns clogging the sight lines, tripping over the power cords, or screaming into the cathedral ceilings that echo and garble their words, you're doomed.

Here are some physical conditions to avoid if possible:

- Stages situated in front of big windows or some other glass barrier that allows passersby to peer in and make faces behind the performers.

- Performing areas that are neither fully joined to nor completely separated from other sections of the bar or restaurant allowing the bar noise, the hoots and hollers of the sports fanatics, or the clank and clunk of table chatter to spill over and mangle the performance.

- Restaurants in general! Spoken word performances are not background music. They require active audiences. It's hard for some folks to eat spaghetti and enjoy a sonnet at the same time.

- Open areas like food courts or student union lobbies where peripheral traffic pulls focus from the stage.

- Stages in odd places like on the top of a portable hot dog stand. (Don't laugh, I've been there. Done that. And I hope I'm not going back for more.)

- Venues with nooks and crannies where patrons can hide and talk loud.

- Oddly shaped venues that divide the seating area so portions of the audience cannot see or hear each other.

After you've let your vision guide your choice of venue, you'll most likely have to let the venue's physical realities revise the specifics of your show. A perfect match is rare. You can't write elaborate costume changes into the script if the club has no backstage. You can't have a troupe of tap-dancing poets on a 4-by-4-foot plywood stage covered with a rug.

But don't let the physical nature of a venue limit your creativity without a fight. At the Green Mill, we've done costume changes in the restrooms and we've moved the tables back for the swashbuckling Swordsmen of verse who whisked rapiers above the heads of eye-popping patrons while reciting sonnets to damsels in distress. Push the limitations as far as you can, but realize the limitations of the space you're creating in.

I

A Rapier Man did love a Queen,
He loved her right and true
Alas, she could not love him back,
Her heart turned black and blue.

He goes off to fight the Spaniards for his beloved Queen. And in the midst of battle...

XII

Love's beauty overwhelmed him
"O England" he did cry
"I want my Queen to be mine own
Or else here I should die!"

And a Spanish crossbow lets loose a shaft which didth strike home and cause the Rapier Man to stumble over the battlement and...

XVII

Here lies a gallant Rapier Man
His tomb a sea of green
His limbs accrushed, a sword abroke
He died for Love of Queen.

—from "Thrust for Glory" a ballad by Dirk Perfect (www.theswordsmen.com)

What About the Stage?

When you envision your slam, what does stage look like? Are you thinking black-box intimacy, storefront theater, or out-of-the-box under-the-moonlight stadium seating? Are your imaginary performers belting out verse on a bandstand or a space cleared on the dance floor?

Staging is a big consideration, before, during, and after your choice of venue, so we devoted a separate chapter to it. To find out more about your stage options, check out Chapter 8, "All the Slams a Stage."

Checking for Essentials: Necessary Services

You can't expect your audience to sit through three hours of performance poetry if they're not physically comfortable, fed and watered, and able to use the restroom occasionally. Check to be sure that the venue has all the services you need and expect—adequate restrooms, decent food (at least some bar nuts or potato chips), refreshing beverages (beer, cocktails, decent coffee, and/or soft drinks at prices nobody's gonna squawk about) and several payment options (cash, debit, Visa, MasterCard, American Express, barter in poetry books).

Maybe you want a place to set up a concession stand, a prep room, or an establishment that provides stagehands to move furniture, its own lights, and a sound system along with someone to run it. The more a venue provides in-house, the less you have to haul in.

Location, Location, Location

If you open a snow cone stand in Alaska, don't expect long lines to cue up for your cool, refreshing Italian Ice. Similarly, when scoping out potential venues, location should be near the top of your list.

In major urban centers it's a big plus if your venue is located near convenient public transportation, easy to find, and in a fairly safe neighborhood (only a few drive-bys now and then). It's an even bigger plus if parking is nearby and free. Being situated in the high profile framework of a hip new artsy business district can add a couple points. And chalk up a couple more points for lots of pedestrian traffic and a dynamic nightlife.

The slam qualifies as an offbeat art form, so people will travel to seek it out. That's part of the fun. But the easier you make it for them, the more assured you can be that they'll return week after week.

Write All This Down

Your wish list is growing, but it's only floating around in your brain. And if you're anything like me, your brain is not the most reliable storage facility. Jot down your criteria and look it over. Save your memory for memorizing poems. Get fixated. Make a chart. You can burn the evidence later. A criteria list in black and white is worth much more than one bouncing around like a pinball in your noodle. Your list should address the following key categories plus any other issues you find important:

- Size
- Clientele
- Ambience
- Location
- Performance Area
- Customer Comforts and Services
- Owner Personality

When you're heading out for a night on the town, stick a notepad and a pencil in your pocket, so you can jot down information about potential slam hot spots. Sure, you might look a little geeky, but when you emerge from your drunken stupor, you'll be able to recount where you've been...assuming, of course, you had the wherewithal to write it down.

At the Sound of Ohhmmm, Begin the Search

Now that you have a detailed list of venue criteria, crumple it up and toss it. You're a poet. Poets don't do lists. Yeah yeah, I just told you to go compulsive and write things down, and that was a necessary stage in the process. But now that you've taken the rational approach, allow the irrational to show you how silly lists can be. Take the Zen approach. Feel the force. The place is going to find you.

Of course, if that's a little too loosey-goosey welcome-to-the-sixties for you, dig that crumpled criteria list out of the trash, smooth the wrinkles, and use the list to create one or two additional lists of spaces that smack of potential. The following sections highlight various ways of searching for and locating prospective slam venues.

Finger Walking

One of the easiest ways to spot prospective venues doesn't even require you to leave your home or apartment. You probably have some newspapers lying around—gather them up. Grab your phone book—the yellow pages. See if you have any neighborhood newsletters hidden under your bed or lying on the bathroom floor.

Check the entertainment sections of the newspapers and write down (or circle, if you're lazy like me) every venue ad or listing that seems to fit your criteria. Check for bookstores, nightclubs, libraries, cultural institutions, and any other places that sound promising–don't forget to include in your notes names, addresses, and phone numbers.

The Net Search

Many newspapers, libraries, bookstores, TV and radio stations, city governments, cultural foundations, and poetry organizations have calendars on their websites listing community events of an artistic and entertainment nature. Pull up those sites and figure out where the happenings are happenin' in your town or city. Cut and paste an e-list together. Surf where the surfing leads you, and write down or print out event names, dates, and times.

Hit the Pavement

You've been cooped up too long making lists. You're a creative artist. You need fresh air, trees, moonlight. Oh! There's the library; it's still open. Lucky thing you've got your criteria notes in your pocket. Check the bulletin board. Any poetry readings? Any venue possibilities? Check out the basement, just in case.

Hey wait, don't go home yet. Get a cup of coffee at the Café Mocha Loca. They have a bulletin board, too. And the art gallery. And the theaters. And look! There's a flyer in the window of that grocery store.

Did you talk with the librarian? The coffee counter person? The cashier? Go back. Now is not the time to act shy. You're on a mission.

Okay, you're tired. Go home. But if you didn't write this all down, you're gonna have to do it again tomorrow. If you did log your discoveries, you've got a very good grip on what's available around and about your town, and you can take a well-deserved nap.

Hook Up with Your Connections

Searching for and exploring venue candidates can be exhilarating, but sometimes the most efficient way to track down top venues is to pick up the phone and network. Call people you know in the arts and entertainment fields. Call your party-animal friends—the ones who go clubbing every weekend. Call people you don't know and get phone numbers of people they know.

People love to help other people. I get calls from strangers from all over world, asking advice on how to start a slam. You never know where your next lead will come from. Sometimes the person you call can't help you directly, but they know a person who knows a person who can. In addition to helping you gather the information you need, talking to folks spreads the word that you're going into the slam business, and people will start contacting *you*.

Judgment Day

You've got a collection of criteria and a list of possibilities. You're ready to let that venue find you. You're going to know without looking at your list, but grab the list anyway (the one I told you to crumple up) and take the following steps to zoom in on the perfect venue:

1. Arrange your list of potential candidates by location, most desirable to least.
2. Check to see which venues are available on the evenings you hope to stage your show. For instance if your plan is to have a weekly show on Mondays, and the place is closed on Mondays... scratch it off the list.
3. See if any other criteria eliminate venues before taking the next big step. Scratch these losers off your list, leaving no more than six prospects. (Scratch lightly; you might need that list if your top six prospects fall through.)
4. Check out the six best locations that survived your cuts.

What Night's Right?

Once you've hit on the right venue or narrowed your list down to three or four promising candidates, pick a night for your show. For obvious reasons, Fridays and Saturdays are the best nights for attracting an audience.

Unfortunately, they're also the most competitive nights for entertainment. You not only compete with regular weekly shows, but also with all kinds of special concerts that come to town for weekend engagements. And there's going to be pressure from the venue owner for you to prove yourself in prime time. So which days are best?

- **Monday:** This is down time for most bars and nightclubs. The good news is that the owner might let you try out your newfangled poetry show—what's she got to lose? The bad news is that people might not overcome Monday night inertia and leave the house, especially during football season when you'll be contending with Monday Night Football and other modern American attention-grabbers.

- **Tuesday:** Like Monday, Tuesday is usually an off day. Bring in a steady crowd on a Monday or Tuesday and the venue owner will kiss your poetic feet.

- **Hump Day:** Wednesday is generally a good day for poetry performances, because they usually don't become party hardy affairs... usually. Folks drop in, have a couple drinks, and get home at a reasonable hour.

- **Thursday:** Like Friday and Saturday, Thursday can be a long night out for lots of people. They figure they can fake a half-day Friday no matter how frazzled they become on Thursday night.

- **Friday:** Great night, lots of excitement, but generally too much competition. If an owner (and an audience) has a choice between your poetry slam show and a top touring rock band, guess who's going to win?

- **Saturday:** See Friday.

- **Sunday:** Like Monday and Tuesday, Sunday is an off night, but it's still weekend time. I've had pretty good success with my Sunday night show.

The Initial Reconnaissance

Your first visit to a prospective venue should ideally be on the night you'd like to hold your show. If you're a nerd, put your criteria list on a clipboard and have check boxes in front of each item. If you're like me, forget to take the criteria list. Go to the place, order something tasty and observe. Observe the clientele, the service staff, the entertainment, and how you feel about the joint. If you get good vibes, find out who the manager is and/or meet the owner. If you're shy about this, join the club. It's perfectly natural. The reaction you get from the owner will tell you a lot about whether you want to stage your show there.

I stopped by the Get Me High Jazz Club almost a dozen times before speaking to Butchie, the owner, about doing my first show there. An obstacle to speaking to Butchie was that I didn't think he could talk. He always communicated by snapping his fingers like some Gone Hipster from the Beat Age. When he finally did speak, it shocked me, but it also opened the door to the Monday Night readings.

Don't Jump before You Have To

Keep in mind that this strategic perusal is not about making a decision. You're there to sense the vibe. You can also sneak that criteria list out of your pocket and check things off while nobody's looking. If you walked in with a clipboard, the owner or a loyal regular has probably already thrown you out or made you so uncomfortable that you had to leave.

Back home after you've looked at the top six prospects, compare the specifics of each. Is that intuition percolating? If nothing's blowin' your skirt up, grab your list and highlight the next top six. If none of the possibilities pan out, pack your bags and come to Chicago.

Closing the Deal

Hopefully your skirt *did* fly up, and you've narrowed down your options to choices A and B. You've met the owners from both and maybe casually mentioned the idea you have in your head. It's time to make it happen. Choice A is way better than choice B, but B could work. So go to B first and practice. But before you're ready to talk turkey, read the fine print and iron out the details, as explained in the next sections.

Money Talk

Nowadays you don't have to go begging a venue owner to allow you the use of his back room for your poetry show. Poetry, spoken word, and slams are now respected forms of entertainment. Club owners and presenters in all categories often seek out well-known slam organizers to create new and special events for them. So don't grovel—you have something of value to offer.

Here are a variety of money deals often agreed upon for club work.

- **A Cut of the Door:** This is a low-end deal. You as the show maker or slammaster get a percentage of the cover charged at the door. If your show draws a big drinking crowd filling the cash register for the owner, this is a lousy deal. But if it's the best you can get, take it. It's better than you paying them to use their space, which happens more often than it should.

- **Full Door:** The full cover charge goes in your pocket, and the club makes its money off the big-spending crowd you attract. This is the standard club deal and it's fair for both sides. An added expense on your part may be that the club will require you to provide a door person to collect the money, but this isn't always the case.

- **Full Door Plus:** If you attract a huge crowd, you might be able to negotiate a cut of the money made off food and beverage sales. Ask the owner to add a dime or a quarter to the cost of drinks during your performances. The club doesn't lose, as long as people keep buying, and you pocket a little extra change to cover expenses.

- **Guaranteed Minimum:** For special shows and one night stands (especially touring shows), ask for a guaranteed minimum against the door charge. This means that the venue will pay you a minimum amount, say $200 of the total take. If more than $200 is collected at the door, you get the full door. But if less than $200 is collected the owner makes up the difference. This is sometimes combined with the percentage scenario mentioned above to make it more balanced.

- **A Flat Fee:** For institutional work and some club arrangements, negotiate a flat fee. They pay you an agreed upon amount, you show up and do a show. This sometimes requires a contract and negotiations to nail down all the specifics: load-in time, lighting and sound requirements, length of performances, lodging, travel expenses...M&Ms backstage with wine, cheese, and finger sandwiches?

You're going to have to work your way up the pay scale. You might have to start out very low ($500 for a two-hour show featuring a band and four slammers), but if your show gains a fine reputation in the concert circles it's not a false illusion to dream that some day you could earn $10,000 or more for the same show, polished to perfection, of course.

- **Pass the Hat:** Many clubs and coffee shops have a pass-the-hat policy, sometimes because laws restrict them from charging admission and sometimes because that's the way they prefer to do business. Volunteer donations, of course, go up and down depending on the quality of the performance, but even with the best shows, total "tips" are unpredictable. If you can get a better deal than pass the hat, do so.

Who Does What?

Everything about the 1999 NPS in Chicago was ringing bells and invoking high fives all around. We had more audience than could fit into the preliminary night venues. Great performances. A *60 Minutes* film crew was roaming the streets catching the fever and action. Saturday night finals lay ahead.

I had my checklist on my clipboard crossing off the to-dos. It was hectic, but things were getting done. Ten minutes before curtain, the union stage manager for the glamorous historically restored Chicago Theater, where all the greats dating back to vaudevillian days have played, asks me where our cue caller for the light changes was. "Our what?" "Your cue caller." "I gave the light guy the script." "He just throws the switch, someone on your side calls the cues." "Oh sh...."

Luckily, Danny Solis, famed slam elder from Albuquerque stepped up to handle those light cues like a pro. The curtain went up and the show was magnificent.

> "Killer Elephant Rampages Honolulu!"
> the headline said.
> At first I thought it was a joke,
> the elephant caught in front page ink,
> gaudy circus head gear still in place.
> Then,
> I saw the streaks of blood,
> death's red fingers
> wrapped
> around another fleshy frame.
> —from "Elephant Song" by Danny Solis

Every detail illuminated in this chapter has or should have a human being attached to it, and it's your job as slammaster or show maker to be sure the bodies are present and they know what to do. Some duties are covered by the venue management, some not. Get it down in black and white, even if it's just a hard nose spoken agreement in clear understandable language. Every detail has to be attended to; if it's not, the curtain could go up without the lights going on.

Hey! I Can't Find a Venue!

"That's right, there's nothing and no place in my town! Watching the streetlights go on is the highlight of the evening. I'm doomed. I'll have to move to the big city. Peapod, Pennsylvania, is going to remain slamless."

Hold on. A few rocks remain unturned.

You have an apartment don't you? Have a house party slam. Start it low key with an eye toward renting an abandoned storefront. There's got to be a church basement left vacant at least one night every couple weeks. Come on, did you check out the library? Every town's got a library.

When you boil it down, it's not the space that makes a slam gyrate; it's the people versifying and populating in it. If you've got people, you've got the main ingredient for a slam. Anywhere is better than nowhere.

If you remember anything, remember...

- A venue should be large enough to accommodate the patrons but small enough to generate the excitement of a happening.

- The ambience of a venue is a critical element in ensuring the success of a show.

- Choose a venue that's conveniently located where you're more likely to attract the audience you desire.

- Compose a list of criteria for the ideal venue to give yourself a method for sizing up the options objectively.

- Once you have narrowed your list of prospective venues down to two or three, talk to the owners and see if you can strike a reasonable deal.

- Anywhere is better than nowhere.

NEXT UP!

Worse Than Nothing: Bad Scenes

If you remember anything, remember...

8 ALL THE SLAM'S A STAGE

All the world may be a stage, but some parts of it get more focus than others. And that's what a stage is for—to draw focus, to give heightened importance to what takes place upon it. Sure a single voice bellowing like a red-faced clown in the bustle of a city street can draw focus, if the voice is strong enough and the antics compelling, but performing over an assemblage of chattering humanity can be a losing battle. On the other hand, a whispered stanza at the footlights of a proscenium stage can hush a thousand people.

From the morality pageants of medieval times to the extravaganzas of the Roman Colosseum to the outrageous spectacles of Marilyn Manson, performers, producers, directors, and slammasters have had to make clear choices concerning the creative use of spaces and stages. When you get down to the nitty gritty of deciding how to present your show or shows, you'll be dealing with all kinds of platforms, stages, and surprises.

This chapter describes the most common setups and conditions. Each has its purpose. Each has its problems. As a show maker, you'll need to be aware of all of them and the options surrounding them.

Poet-in-a-Box: The Black Box

One of the most potent "stages" a performance poet encounters is the black box—a small, intimate, flexible theater space with walls, floor, and ceiling painted black. It's sort of like those boxes used for puppet shows, only people play in them. Stadium style seating is commonly found in the black box, but moveable chairs are often used so that the seating and performance area can be moved anywhere in the room. With the right lighting, the black box enables a performance poetry presentation to attain a mesmerizing intimacy and a subtle power unachievable in most nightclub or coffeehouse settings.

> The history of the physical stage dates back to ancient times. The evolution and diversity of stage structures are directly related to the forms of theater presented on them and how they best serve the mobility of the players and the plot.

By its nature, the black box attaches a more theatrical ambience to an evening and heightens audience expectations. In the box, a performer's every word will be scrutinized like never before. Success in the black box depends upon carefully selecting show components that suit the nature of the black box without sacrificing the open and informal qualities that make slams resonate.

To assess whether a black box is right for you, ask yourself the following questions (and answer them, too):

- **Does your show's vision fit the black box ambience?** If the crystal ball vision that's materializing in your head reveals scruffy open mic poets kibitzing with each other in a "Hello, there. Howdy! Whatsup?" revelry as they bump their way up to the stage while hecklers boogaloo in the aisles, a black box might not be the appropriate spot for your anything-goes scenario.

- **How's the seating arranged?** Remember a black box sometimes offers flexibility in seating and sometimes not, but seating must always focus audience attention like a laser beam on the poet performer. In a black box, people sit down for one purpose, and one purpose only—to see the show. You can minimize distractions and control focus by arranging and rearranging the seating.

- **Are you planning to include music?** Acoustic and very laid-back amplified music can add the right touch to the black box ambience. A big brassy orchestra will blow heads off shoulders.

- **Is there enough room?** Black box theater spaces are small, holding twenty-five to one hundred and fifty max. If you're planning a "Slam Spectacular" with ten teams bussed in from around the country competing in a one-night marathon performance, bury the box. Very focused ensemble work and solo shows work best in a black box. If you're hoping to sell 300 tickets, forget about it.

Above the Crowd on the Bandstand

Commonly found in most clubs and in some coffeehouses, the bandstand is the performance poet's most familiar stage setting. The platform is typically several inches to a few feet above floor level.

Positioned high up with the bright lights shining on your countenance may be exhilarating, but the pin-spot reality of the situation is that the higher the stage climbs, the more disconnected from the audience a performer feels. Intimacy is sacrificed for the elevated "see me" bandstand three or four feet off the floor. When you consider whether the bandstand is going to play well for your show, check the following:

- **Line of sight:** You want everyone in the venue to be able to see the performances without craning their necks or having to sit on their friends' shoulders. For a thrash band, it doesn't matter much if the crowd can't see the guitar player smash his axe against the bass player's amp. However, a big part of a spoken word performance is the poet's physical presence on the stage. Imagine only hearing (not seeing) Othello's final speech from outside in the lobby of the local Globe Theatre. For the most part an elevated bandstand almost always improves line of sight, but check anyway.

It is much more difficult for an audience to comprehend vocal communication when unable to see a performer's lips. For this reason, actors are always directed to speak with more volume and slightly over-emphasized enunciation when their backs are turned to the audience.

- **Level of intimacy:** The higher the performer rises above the crowd, the less intimate the connection. Imagine Romeo, oh Romeo, trying to embrace his Juliet while she's standing on a kitchen table and he's on his knees by the dog bowl. This might be kinky fun for some, but it's sure not an intimate connection. It's tension. At some point, Juliet, sweet Juliet, must descend from her heights and make good on the intimacy Romeo and the audience long for. It's a tradeoff; you want the performer to be as close to audience as possible while still being visible to all.

Most bandstands come equipped with beaucoup lighting and sound capabilities and are very slammer friendly. They can range in size from a cramped 4-by-4 foot inverted plywood box to a huge steel reinforced platform 20 feet across and 15 feet deep, and beyond—think of those enormous stages erected in the ball parks at all those Big Time Rock Star concerts you've attended, the true American bandstands.

The Spartan Stage: Cleared Space

Many times slammers find themselves performing in bookstores, coffeehouses, and multi-purpose rooms where the stage consists of floor space cleared of the usual furniture that occupies it. Be careful that whoever reconfigures the room has at least a smidgen of theater sense and hasn't placed his idea of a-good-spot-to-perform in front of a marble staircase or in the dreariest corner of a cluttered bookstore.

Cleared space is not conducive to highly dramatic material. If you're performing in cleared space, it's best to go super-casual—try a little Billy Clinton, town-hall meeting, gift-of-gab (and grab) approach, and if you're about to go highly dramatic on them, qualify it with a "Hey, hold on to your cushions; I'm going to shift gears a little and drive into performance mode now. It might be a little scary for a minute or so. Don't panic. I won't hurt you. It's just the slam."

The Great Hall

A variation on the Spartan space is the Great Hall. During the Renaissance and medieval times the King, Queen, and their court were entertained while seated at a long banquet table in a rectangular room—the Great Hall, with entrances at each of the four corners. Jugglers, dancers, jesters, and troubadours entered from the various points of the compass to gain the favor of the court with their performances.

When you're faced with staging a performance in a rather sterile meeting room or hotel conference hall, you might be able to transform a potential "poetry lecture" into a courtly banquet. Don't bring shanks of pork in, just position your poets around the room and have them feign grand entrances into the Great Hall flourishing their words and juggling their syllables. You might not want to keep this up for forty minutes, but to start the show and accent it now and then, or put a befitting closer on it, it could be just the right elixir for a savory meal of acrobatic verse.

The Big-Time Stage: The Proscenium

Big-time performances, such as the championship bouts of the national slam, are almost always held on a proscenium stage. These are the stages you're accustomed to seeing when you attend a Broadway play, opera, or ballet. The stage is typically at or below the audience level with theater seating in front of it. In some cases, an orchestra pit stands between the stage and the audience. The audience views the action through the proscenium archway that frames the main area where actors act, dancers dance, and slammers slam. The great thing about the proscenium is that it typically comes equipped with great lighting, a fantastic sound system, and prestige.

Bring on the Bells and Whistles

To make the big stage work, your show needs big BIG! visuals. Props, backdrops, lots of people on the boards all at once, lighting that changes moods and isolates areas, blocking (stage movement) that makes maximum use of the space. Think of figure skating champions and how they cover the expanse of the rink, circles of light following them as they spray shaved ice to a halt in one corner and then glide gracefully across to another. When you're on the big stage, plan a big show that uses every square foot of it.

Bigger's Not Always Better

As slammaster, the proscenium might seem like the ideal arrangement for your really big show, a perfect opportunity to stage the ultimate happening. But you'd better back up a moment! The proscenium is often too large and too formal to generate super-charged, shoulder-to-shoulder excitement. In 1999 we held the final night of the National Slam at the massive Chicago Theater, and even though we filled the main floor with 2,500 bodies, we never attained that busting-at-the-seams feel. The balcony and lobby area could have held 3,000 more. It was a great, great show but not Woodstock revisited.

Part of the reason that many slam poets have drifted toward using overly rhetorical language in their texts is because they often find themselves orating on proscenium stages on the final nights of national competitions. It takes far more skill and experience to engage an audience with lyrical poetics from a proscenium than it does to unleash the fury of a speechmaker.

The Outdoor Stage: Help!

Sooner or later, if you've been gigging it hard year after year, you're going to end up on an outdoor stage performing at the Dawn-to-Dusk Bird & Bat Word Fest or (by the mayor's invitation) at the Grand Opening of the new city library. At first you're going to say yippie! But hold that yip. Sure, you've been to lots of outdoor festivals and envied the rockabilly bands cranking it out for hordes of crazed fans who swing dance their way up to the elevated platform like they're going to see the Memphis Boy rotating his hips from the great beyond. But I guarantee that you'll have a different attitude once you've experienced the far-away feeling you get facing a crowd that seems more like a sea of cliché faces than flesh-and-blood humanity.

Speak Up, They Can't Hear Ya!

Outdoor work is tough. You're generally performing on either a permanent (concrete usually) outdoor facility, like a band shell or a gazebo, or on temporary stages erected especially for the current event. And many times there is no stage, just a tent and folding chairs, maybe a riser that elevates the performer six to eight inches above the grass. In any event, expect the permanent outdoor space to suck—it might be architecturally beautiful, but acoustically it's a nightmare.

The great outdoors swallows sound. A tree could fall onstage and nobody would hear it. Nearly every outdoor stage I've performed on chewed up my words and puked them back at everybody like cold mashed potatoes. And you can imagine how enthusiastically the audience gobbled them up.

Temporary outdoor staging can be even worse. It elevates and frames you into a proscenium picture, which is good, but the open sky above you does little to help the passersby focus on you. And if the lighting and sound fall through, you're sunk. Without sound amplification and good (colorful) lighting, you're just another body on the stage. "Hey dere, is that the stagehand or the sound technician?... Oh, it's the poet. Sorry."

Think Big

As with the big proscenium stage, to make an outdoor situation work, your show demands big visuals, movement, music, and strong animated performances. The music draws the focus of the passing crowds, and once they're engaged, a dynamic performer in the spotlight can hold their attention... for a while, anyway. It's best to mix in ensemble work or slammers performing with the music. If you're holding a competition as part of the show, play up the pomp and pageantry of it. Be sure the slammers dress the part. Put some giant scoreboards on the stage. Think big outside and maybe you can keep from being swallowed by that big open sky.

Many performers, musicians, and troupes are experienced in performing at outdoor festivals. And many of these have a spoken word/poetic element to them. Jugglers, acrobats, circus performers, and dada artists have all participated in slam shows I've staged in difficult open-air facilities. They know how to compel even the most scattered crowd to listen.

The Rickety Rent-a-Stage

Beware of rental stages, especially the low-rent variety. On a cheap rent-a-stage you feel like you're standing in a rowboat bobbing about on choppy seas. If you romp around on the shaky platform, everything that isn't nailed down teeters, totters, and usually falls. And if that's not enough to unnerve even the steadiest performer, the microphone picks up every audible thump and clump that sounds when you step too hard on the some-assembly-required stage. If you have an elaborate dance-the-poem routine blocked out and see that you're going to be performing it on a flimsy platform, tone it down to finger dancing and hand gestures.

If you're a slammaster planning that big show with elephant props and giant flip-flopping word acrobats, spend a little extra bread and get high quality equipment, or be sure that the promoter who contracted the elephantine show has lined up a solid platform.

You can find some high-quality rental stages and seating. Just go on the Web and use your favorite search engine to look for "rental stage," or grab your handy-dandy yellow pages and look under "event planning." Or talk to local festival organizers and find out who they use.

What? No Stage?! No Cleared Space?!

When you were skipping from venue to venue on your initial search for your slam's home, you probably encountered at least one joint where you begin to think, "Why do I think this place might work? Where are the poets supposed to perform? Nix this place. It has no stage, no clearing in the woods. Not even an X taped to the floor to show where performers should stand." Of course, this is totally unacceptable, but the manager's cute, the owner's gung-ho, there's a flock of people crying "We Want the Slam!" so your only recourse is to make it work:

- Find an area with some decent lighting and where the audience can see you, shove the tables aside, scrounge up some crates to stand on, and let 'er rip!

  Or

- Make the whole room your stage! Whatever you do, do it in a way that's not going to rattle the owner and in a way that makes it look planned.

If your weekly or monthly venue comes with no stage, nail some 2-by-6's to the perimeters of a 4-by-4 sheet of ¾ inch plywood, paint it black, staple some carpeting to the top of it, and bingo—Broadway, you've got your own portable stage. Just make sure it'll hold a good-sized performer jumping up and down as if on a trampoline.

Worse Than Nothing: Bad Scenes

Although the complete lack of a performance area is a definite bummer, other stage options that seem workable at first glance can be steel traps waiting to snap. The following list describes some setups you would be wise to avoid:

- A stage behind the bar top and bartender. That might be a safe place if you're doing a striptease, but for a poetry performance, it's like being a monkey in the zoo. And when the bartender starts shaking martinis all is lost.

- A very high proscenium with an open, unoccupied orchestra pit hugging its edge. Again, the distance from the crowd makes this less than attractive. And there's always a chance that in the midst of a passionate stanza you'll fall into the pit.

- In front of any entranceway to the outside or an adjacent room—swinging doors, revolving doors, any doors. Every time a new patron comes in and looks up at the performer, the audience watches the unplanned drama. Even if the door never opens, the expectation that it might open can often draw more attention than your act.

- Boats, football fields, ski jumps, and so on. Unless you've reached the star status of a rock legend or a Hollywood film idol, avoid them. On second thought, never attempt it.

The "His" n "Hers" doors at the Green Mill adjacent to the stage are an avoidable distraction depending on who has to use them and when. For years I've been working them into the act. Many times I've announced the next open mic poet and they instantly and unexpectedly emerged from the restroom for their unplanned grand entrance.

If you remember anything, remember...

- The right stage draws a room's focus to the performer, providing an essential element for the success of a performance.

- Different types of stages have evolved over time to accommodate different performance needs.

- Slammasters should anticipate encountering a wide variety of stages and performance spaces from the tiny black box to huge outdoor rental stages.

- To ensure the success of your performance, try to secure stages that best accommodate the style of your planned show, and when that's not possible, tailor performances to fit the space.

- Stages that have the potential of drawing the audience focus away from the performer can often be worse than no stage at all.

NEXT UP!

Tuning In Sound Systems—Can You Hear Me Now?

Omni- or Unidirectional Microphones
Microphone Stands
Four-Channel Mixer
Graphic EQ Settings
Speakers & Speaker Location
Monitors

Light 'Em If They Got 'Em

Lights Up, Lights Down
Homespun Lighting Systems
Top-Shelf Lighting

Puttin' Out the Glitz

Dressing Up the Poets & Stage
Back-Up Beats, Styles, & Rhythms
Slide Shows
Props and Drops

If you remember anything, remember...

9 LET'S GET TECHNICAL

A good stage, well-suited to a particular performance, can frame your show and focus your audience's attention in the right direction. But without proper lighting and quality sound amplification, even the best stage can seem like a vacant lot at midnight. If it's dark up there, you might try holding a flashlight beam on Sally Slammer's lovely face, but your arm is going to droop after thirty minutes. If you're running an open mic and the shiest, most inexperienced slam virgins are eager to "do it" for the first time, you're going to need a microphone to catch their whispers and a powered mixer to send their amplified jitters through the speakers to the hecklers thirty rows back.

If you're lucky, the venue itself will have all the required tech equipment in place when you arrive. They might even provide you or one of your cohorts with a brief tutorial on how to adjust it during the show. When you're not so lucky, turn to this chapter for coping strategies—how to manipulate and manage a sound system, how to deal with stage lighting, and how to introduce costumes, props, and other window dressing add-ons that make your show technically tight.

Tuning In Sound Systems—Can You Hear Me Now?

Nothing can knock the power out of a great performance faster than the piercing screech of feedback or the garbled tones of a defective soundboard. Spoken word artists require more precise sound amplification than singers and way better than rock groups. As a slammaster, you're going to encounter many different situations, from sound systems so complex they require professional engineers to man them to no sound system at all requiring you to provide your own.

Whether you're heading down to Barnie's Sound Amplification Emporium to rent speakers, microphones, and amplifiers for your Limerick Slam or inspecting the in-house system at the Blue Gator Club, you'll need to be familiar with the characteristics and components of a quality sound system discussed in the following sections.

Omni- or Unidirectional Microphones

All microphones are not created equal. Unidirectional microphones reduce the *off-access sound*—sounds to the side and back of microphone, such as audience chatter or mumbles from the performer next to you—and generally are preferable for spoken word performances. The Shure 57 is a good choice. It's the workhorse of the industry. The one drawback to the unidirectional microphone is that it tends to boost the bass, causing the percussion to pop. Omnidirectional microphones are better at picking up sounds from several sources.

Don't forget the cables. The industry standard is a three-prong type known as XLR, but you'll occasionally run into microphones and soundboards that use a ¼ plug or some other oddball connection. Be sure to check the system and microphones you're using and secure compatible cables for it.

Microphone Stands

It might sound like a no-brainer that you need microphone stands, but believe me, on more than a few occasions the club or cultural center supposedly providing a complete sound system didn't have microphone stands or the clips that screw into the stand to saddle the microphones. If you're in charge of the sound setup, make sure you have a stable microphone stand that's easy to adjust.

A six- to eight-inch gooseneck attachment screwed onto the top of the microphone stand can be of great benefit during the open-mic. Rather than struggling with the height adjustments of the stand itself (usually over tightened by the last performer or broken by an aggressive musician/poet/madman with ham hands) the performers or emcee simply bend the gooseneck up or down to the desired height.

Four-Channel Mixer

Powered mixers mix and amplify the sound received through the microphones and send it out through the speakers. Unpowered mixers require a separate amplifier to drive the speakers. It's best to have at least four channels on the mixer, one for each microphone, musical instrument, and/or other gadget you intend to plug in, plus a spare in case a channel goes dead in the middle of a performance. Each channel should have, at the very least, a dial for high-, mid-, and low-range frequencies, a dial for gain (volume), and a slide adjustment for minor tweaking the volume. High-end boards have lots of other buttons and switches for reverb, monitors, muting, and so on.

If you're renting a system, let your needs and your budget guide your choice. A quality six-channel board, two speakers, four microphones, stands, and cords can be delivered to your show on the night of the performance for as little as $250. Of course, the cost can soar into the thousands if you get carried away.

Graphic EQ Settings

The sound equipment in many clubs, theaters, and concert halls often includes a row of sliding levers stretched across a grid of a dozen or so sound frequencies for equalizing (EQing) the system. The function of these levers is to tune the system to the room's acoustic characteristics, but many clubs allow bands to change the Graphic EQ settings for individual performances. If the tonal quality coming out of the speakers remains muffled and indistinct no matter how carefully you adjust the channel dials for high-, mid-, and low-range frequencies, the problem could be in the Graphic EQ settings. Before messing with them yourself, ask the club manager for assistance, and pray that he knows what he's doing.

Speakers & Speaker Location

Those canned speakers embedded in the ceiling of the library aren't going to hack it. You'll need woofers and tweeters more akin to the big black boxes you've seen hanging from the upper piping of a bandstand or on pole supports flanking the concert stage. Two speakers are always better than one. Models from Jbl, EON, or Sampson are good choices. Somebody's guitar or bass amp won't do the trick. Slams are about sound, good sound for great words. Don't skimp on the speakers.

> Double Warning! As I indicated above, beware of in-house PA systems with speakers embedded in the ceiling—the kind you find at convention centers or in hospitals. These systems are not made to produce quality sound. They are designed to carry information, not art. Avoid using them and know that if you do use them, the performance will suffer.

Speaker location can drastically affect the tonal quality of what comes out of them. Feedback (that awful ear-drum-blowing screech) is caused by the amplified sound coming out of the speakers and feeding back through the microphone—think of it as sound amplified to the infinite power. If the speakers are placed directly behind or too close to the microphones, they're going to create feedback. It's always best to situate them a little forward of the microphone and above the heads of your performers. Setting the speakers on a bar stool at chest level is better than leaving them on the floor if there's no safe way to hang them high.

Monitors

Monitors are like audio mirrors. They sit onstage facing the performers so the performers can hear what they sound like to the audience. Monitors are not always necessary for spoken word performances, but it's good to have them available if possible. Feeling comfortable with the sound onstage gives a performer confidence, and knowing that the sound you hear onstage is the same as what the audience hears doubles that confidence. If you've ever been bludgeoned by a voice blaring over a loudspeaker, you can bet there are no monitors onstage and the performers don't even realize how nasty loud they are.

Light 'Em If They Got 'Em

More important than a fancy stage, but somewhat less important than the audio quality, is lighting. Lighting can create a stage that's not there. It can set a mood. It can add another creative facet to your show. The right lighting can instantly catapult your poetry event from the dimly lit backstage of another poetry snore into the bright limelight of performance art.

However, you need to use lighting creatively and subtly in order for it to be effective. Don't run out to Ace Hardware, buy a portable floodlight, and assume that blasting your performers with a 200-watt halogen beam will make their performances shine brighter than ever before. They'll just squint through the furnace of light to find you and affix their glare to your forehead. The following sections show you how to put together a quality, low-cost lighting system and use it effectively.

Lights Up, Lights Down

Unless you're dealing with a big theatrical house or concert hall, lighting is going to be basic: lights up and lights down. Controlling the lighting usually is limited to plugging and unplugging cords, flipping on-off switches, or sliding or rotating rheostats to increase or decrease intensity. Sometimes a switch controls only one light. Sometimes it controls a bank of lights. If you're going to change the lighting during your show, someone, preferably a person with a great sense of timing and excellent reflexes, must work the switches.

> White light can often be too harsh for poetry performances. Yellow makes performers look jaundiced. Blue is murky. A combination of colors—white, red, blue, and amber—works best.

Before the show, check the position of the lights to be sure they're pointing to the desired locations. Draft someone to stand onstage where the performers will be and provide feedback as you climb the ladder and nudge the lights to point in the right direction. Between the two of you, you'll know when the lighting is right—when your mock performer's features are sharply illuminated and distinct, and when she stops screaming that the light is burning her eyeballs. Adjusting the lights is pretty simple if the lights are new or well maintained, but adjustments can be tricky if the lights are old and rickety.

Homespun Lighting Systems

For about $50, you can put together an adequate, portable lighting system for your show. Head over to your neighborhood hardware store and purchase four to six clamp-on work lights (which look like silver cones), a few heavy-duty extension cords of various lengths, and some 100-watt red, blue, and amber accent bulbs. For years I've carried five or six of these setups around in the trunk of my car just in case I arrive at a gig to find poor lighting. They've illuminated a dark situation on several occasions. The Green Mill stage has one theater spotlight and four of these homespun pan lights, and it hosts weekly performances of some of the country's top jazz groups, not to mention the most famous of slam shows.

For a string of Chicago Poetry Ensemble performances, the performers were positioned in the audience amidst a network of homespun clamp-on lights. I ran extension cords equipped with on/off switches down the walls to each position. It was a black box situation, total blackout when the house lights went down. The performers used the switched cords to pop on their do-it-yourself spotlights at the appropriate cues.

Top-Shelf Lighting

The big houses, concert halls, and proscenium theaters have complex computerized light boards that control dozens of lights, and some high class nightclubs have several small spotlights that can be moved and focused mechanically with the touch of a button. These conditions almost always carry with them an experienced light technician who is accustomed to working on shows with hundreds of light cues. As elaborate as my poetry shows have been, never have they come close to the complexity of a major theater production or big time rock concert. Trust the light technicians to handle your lighting needs; give them license to be creative, and they will always keep you and your performers properly illuminated. Mistreat them and you might find half your head eclipsed for most of the show.

Puttin' Out the Glitz

Spectacle is one of Aristotle's fundamental elements of drama. Baseball teams use fireworks, get-a-bat days, and be-a-Sumo-wrestler nights to hype the fans. Football uses pass and kick competitions, gyrating cheerleaders, and roaming mascot gags to rile up the rivals. Even Las Vegas energizes its already glitzy neon image with circus tigers and outlandish architectural facades. But Aristotle, whose writings have guided the evolution of drama for more than two thousand years, considered Spectacle to be the least important of the theatrical elements. According to Aristotle, Spectacle is ornamentation to be used sparingly.

Spectacle was a requirement at the Fat Tuesday Celebrations of the Seven Deadly Sins held at Fitzgerald's West Side Poetry Slam in Berwyn, Illinois. Seven poetry ensembles (krewes) created poetry parades modeled after those found on the streets of New Orleans during Mardi Gras. Each krewe represented and expressed sentiments of one of the deadly sins: lust, anger, greed, gluttony, envy, pride, and sloth. Without music, costumes, and spectacle, much of the fun would have been...sinless.

Think of it as a Christmas tree. When you bring it home and stand it up unadorned in the parlor, it's quite a moving experience. It brings the outside in. The pine fragrance supercharges the air. Its presence changes the mood and landscape of the living room into a miracle on Thirty-Fourth Street. Deck the halls, baby!

Then Bobby, the oldest, opens the ornament box and starts pulling out strings of tangled lights, more ornaments, beads, and packets of silver garland. Bobby and the other three kids start bouncing around like SuperBalls in a frenetic sports flick sticking tin soldiers and gold spiders on the low branches, jumping up to toss reindeer near the top. Hey!

Up to a point the extras enhance the natural beauty of the tree, but after too many tosses of tinsel, the magical spirit of the tree disappears under a thick coat of plastic and overdone garland. The moral of the story: There's a fine line between tasteful spectacle and gaudiness; don't cross it.

Dressing Up the Poets & Stage

Costumes are part of most ritual experiences. Every sport has unique, identifiable uniforms. At religious ceremonies, priests and priestesses don ceremonial garb. At graduations, the graduates wear long robes and funny hats. Costumes add to the mystery and meaning of the occasion. They heighten the visual language and help separate the stage experience and its main characters from everydayness. They give the people wearing them importance. They identify the performers as the people to watch, which is especially important when working inside an audience and not strictly onstage.

For a performance at a community college, members of the Bob Shakespeare Poetry Band entered in lavish black performance clothing—not backstage stuff, but in-the-spotlight-glamour garb, embroidered, textured, silky, lacy, sharp. In a review of the show, the local newspaper included a quote from an audience member who said something like, "When those poets in their black outfits came in it was like watching the three villains from that *Superman* flick fly into the room. It rattled me, but I loved it."

Your stage area should don a costume, too, if it's drab and dreary with no character to support the characters on it. Just propping open the top of the grand piano at the Green Mill adds a touch of elegance to the set. Banners and drapes can help frame performers, add a splash of color, and set a mood. A decorated scoreboard or programmed video image used as a backdrop can enhance a tournament's competitive flavors, and can also be used to accent the playfulness of slammin'—imagine slammin' cats being thwarted by mightily slammin' mice racing across the video screen spitting balloons of cat and mice poetics.

The right degree of costuming adds dazzle to a show and performance. Too much can look very silly.

Back-Up Beats, Styles, & Rhythms

Many slams use music to set a preshow mood, as segues between poets, during intermissions, or as an integral part of the night's performances. DJs spin at many slams providing a backbeat for poets and a transition between performers. Live music can be a welcomed break from poet after poet after poet. Singer-songwriters are kinfolk to poets and are often poets themselves. Their performances can deliver a refreshing and inspiring new perspective to a show.

All forms of music have been incorporated into slam shows—rock, folk, jazz, funk, you name it. The opening act at NPS 2002 in Minneapolis was a Native American drum and dance troupe that whirled and stomped and spirited us away to a pre-European wilderness. It was sensational.

Slide Shows

Dateline Chicago: Sunday night. May 10, 1988. Mother's Day. First they load in sound equipment, lots of sound equipment—amps, synthesizers, speakers.

"Hey we've already got speakers at the Green Mill."
"We need extras!" The Loofah Methode had arrived.

"What the heck is a Loofah Methode? And what the heck is all that?"

A procession of film projectors, slide projectors, drummer and drums, sax and sax player, and a 16-foot-wide movie screen parade in through the side door.

"Oh dear! What's next?!"

What came next was a spectacular mix of music, visual projections, props, costumes, and poetry that became a staple of the avant-garde performance art scene (in Chicago) for over a decade. And it all began at the slam.

someone brushed away some dead skin.
held up a mirror, showed me some nerves.
my nerves, exposed, still raw, and gasping for air
like little heads, nostrils flaring, tongues lapping,
at some fresh air.
it was less than a second, less than a second,
and new skin scarred over this aggressive innocence.
less than a second, but i felt the conception take place.
now under my skin
a new life begins.
—from "Loofah Methode" by Cin Salach

Over almost two decades, scores of performers have used visual arts as a backdrop for their verse. One of the most famous of the early slammer/artists who decorated the stage with slides of his iconoclastic art as he punched out his poems, is Tony Fitzpatrick. Tony was the first official referee at the Green Mill, where for a couple years his big Irish mug didn't take no guff from "nobody no how," especially the "art victim poets" who didn't like slammin'. Nobody dared mess with him. If you got a zero, you got a zero. "Now shut up and sit down."

in the dream a jailhouse hand slid out
with a mirror in its fist
and we locked eyes

and the mirror asked You got a cigarette
a tailor-made cigarette
for me?
and do you play chess and could we play?
and could you lay sticks and kindling at my feet
and light me up like a rocket ship?
I want to hold hands with a bomb
and learn how they sing
–from "Hard Angels" by Tony Fitzpatrick
(www.TonyFitzpatrick.com)

Setting up slide projectors at a slam is a relatively easy affair. All you need is an outlet, a table, and a light-colored wall. A well-done slideshow can instantly transform the stale ambience of a room into a snake-charming experience.

Computerized video projections are increasingly replacing old school slide projections especially at European slam events. The 2008 Absolute Poetry Festival (www.absolutepoetry.org) in Montfalcone, Italy, hosted by Lello Voce (www.lellovoce.It) employed a free-styling, in-the-moment video backdrop that changed with (and enhanced) the mood of dozens of spoken word performances.

Props and Drops

Yeah, yeah, we all know about the no-prop rule. That's okay for the national competitions, but I suggest you break the rules now and then for the sake of spectacle by sticking some huge props in the room. Maybe a mannequin representing the dead poet society. Maybe a long-handle hook in the corner to put the fear of humiliation into the hearts of the more pompous open-mic poets. How about a gong?! How about a huge banner with your slam logo on the back wall? Or posters from the national competitions? Maybe drapes of poems pasted together week after week.

For years I would forget to make important announcements at

the Sunday show. It became part of the ritual, part of the spectacle when I started pasting the announcement notes on the support post that occupies the center of the Green Mill. The audience would shout, "Read a note, Marc." It was a great game for the audience while it lasted. Now I can't even remember to paste up the...what was I was suppose to do?

If you remember anything, remember...

- Lighting, sound amplification, and spectacle help draw more precise focus to a performance.

- A unidirectional microphone is best for individual spoken word poetry performances, because it blocks out most background noise.

- Don't place the speakers behind or too close to the microphone, because you'll end up blowing out everybody's eardrums with annoying feedback.

- A little subtle lighting can significantly enhance performances and influence the ambience of a room.

- Add some spectacle to liven up your show and energize the audience, but don't over-season your main course

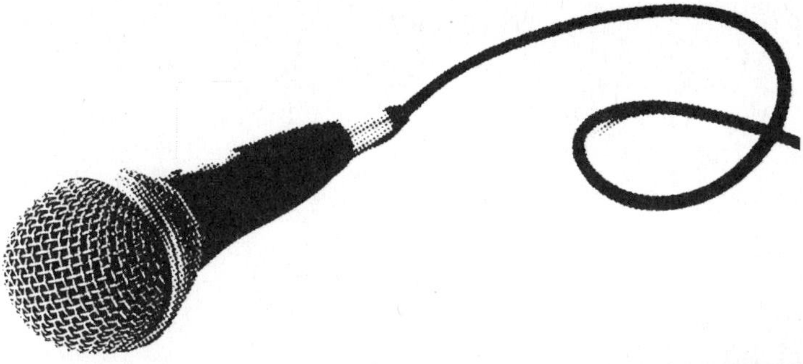

NEXT UP!

Flying Solo

Whipping up a Preshow Checklist
Creating Your Showtime Checklist
Drafting Your Postshow Checklist

Partnerships, Committees, Co-ops, & Chaos

A Partnership of Two or Three
By Committee
Cooperatives
The Three Tier Model—Combining the Best of All Worlds

Help Wanted—Key Positions to Fill…If You Can

Marketing
Scouting and Booking Talented Performance Poets
Emcees Wanted—Charisma Required
Offstage Support

If you remember anything, remember…

10 CHOOSING & ORGANIZING YOUR CREW

Before you fling open the doors to the world premier of your Verb the Earth Slam, you'd better have a reliable staff in place. Without assistants to market the show, line up performers, greet patrons, collect money, manage the sign-up sheet, monitor the sound system, tinker with the lights, babysit the virgin virgins, select and educate scorekeepers, and the all-else that has to be done, you're going to feel like you're playing fifty instruments in a one-(wo)man marching band.

That's not to say it can't be handled solo. I, and many others, have been there and done that, and even enjoyed it. Going solo has some advantages. No worries about when or if the help will show up, no personality conflicts—no one to blame for the mishaps but yourself. And when the show wails, you get all the credit. It's the perfect job for a hyperactive, workaholic control freak.

At some point, however, when the spectacle grows beyond your wildest dreams, you'll *have* to delegate authority and divide up the tasks to keep the big show booming. This chapter shows you how to delegate effectively, efficiently, and without losing control of your mind and the thing you've created.

Flying Solo

You *are* a hyperactive, workaholic control freak, and flying solo is just what makes your cylinders hum. Excellent. Now, strap on every tool and contingency plan your mad hands can get hold of. You're going to need them. You'll be distributing flyers day in and day out, licking stamps whenever you walk out of your poet abode, which is crammed with piles of even more flyers to distribute. You'll be scouting and booking acts instead of sleeping. You'll be haggling with venue owners and managers over the phone and face-to-face. The lights will have to be hung and focused. The chairs unfolded and set. Where are those flippin' microphone stands! Whose got the scorecards and markers?

And if you're fidgeting with the sound system or searching frantically for replacement bulbs and a music stand while patrons are streaming in looking for seats, your show's already headed for trouble, on the rocks before the first simile squeaks out "like, man, pigs squealing" feedback from a misplaced sound monitor.

Whipping Up a Preshow Checklist

Not scared? Okay. Jot down a checklist of everything that needs to be done prior to showtime. This list helps you lay the groundwork, so you're not in a mad scramble when the performers and patrons begin streaming in off the street.

Preshow Checklist

- ❑ Tape up logo banners and show posters
- ❑ Clear stage area
- ❑ Set up microphone stands and plug in mics
- ❑ Turn on sound system and check sound
- ❑ Check and refocus lights
- ❑ Assist back-up band with load-in and setup
- ❑ Sound check band
- ❑ Put sign-up board at entrance door
- ❑ Set up merchandise table

(continued)

- ❏ Give guest list to doorman
- ❏ Set mailing list sign-up cards on tables
- ❏ Set out fish bowl for open mic sign-ups
- ❏ Rehearse opening poem

If the venue has staff in place for collecting money, selling tickets, and seating people, cross those tasks off your list. If you're hosting an outdoor slam and need to build a stage, add that to the list. (See Chapter 8 for more about staging requirements.)

For those of you flying solo *and* taking on the duties of emcee, the importance of a checklist cannot be overemphasized. When showtime hits, you're going to want your mind "in the moment" reacting to and guiding the artistic aspects of the show—not trying to desperately remember what you promised to pay Joey the Mouth or what announcements you wanted to make about your next big project.

Creating Your Showtime Checklist

If you thought the preshow checklist seemed a little over the top, just look at what your show duties include.

Showtime Checklist

- ❏ Greet and seat people
- ❏ Answer questions from newcomers
- ❏ Sign up open mic poets and slam competitors
- ❏ Cue band to get ready for opening music
- ❏ Cue manager to turn down preshow music

(continued)

- ❏ Perform opening poem with band
- ❏ Check on featured performers
- ❏ Answer questions from audience, reporters, etc.
- ❏ Encourage audience to sign mailing lists
- ❏ Introduce open mic poets
- ❏ Adjust volume on mic as necessary for each poet
- ❏ Introduce guest performers
- ❏ Encourage audience to visit merchandise table
- ❏ Monitor merchandise sales
- ❏ Recruit slam judges and scorekeepers
- ❏ Referee slam competition
- ❏ Announce next week's guests
- ❏ Thank the audience for coming
- ❏ Perform closing poem with band

Each of the items on your showtime list may seem like a no-brainer, but in the steam and whistle of a performance they can pile up, build pressure, and cause you to blow a gasket.

Put each simple task, each announcement, each "be sure" on the checklist. Tape it to a wall or on the stage floor. Put a duplicate list in your pocket. Or use index cards with an item or two on each one. Keep the cards in your pocket and toss the card as soon as you've completed the task. However you do it, do it. At some point after many, many shows, all these simple tasks may become automatic, routine, but at the beginning, the smallest slipup could derail an evening.

Drafting Your Postshow Checklist

Done with lists? No! The postshow has some honey-do items, too.

Postshow Checklist

- ❑ Break down sound and lights
- ❑ Help band break down
- ❑ Pay guest performers and band
- ❑ Collect money from merchandise sales
- ❑ Break down merchandise table
- ❑ Pack up unsold merchandise
- ❑ Collect mailing list sign-up cards
- ❑ Take down logo banners and show posters
- ❑ Answer audience questions as you say good-byes
- ❑ Answer interview questions from reporters
- ❑ Collect markers and scorecards
- ❑ Clean up stage
- ❑ Thank manager and service people
- ❑ Final check

And don't forget to make an honest assessment of the event, a list of which performers rocked and which fizzled. At what point did the emcee fail to engage the crowd? How might the lights have been refocused? What paper was that reporter writing for?

If you think you'll remember (without writing them down) all the glitches and hiccups and uncomfortable silences your brain noticed during a show, you're a better slammaster than me. Too many times I've found myself rollicking midway through "next week's" show only to remember, too late, that I should have pushed the front tables farther apart to make a path for the open mic poets to gain access to the stage without having to climb over the recording device which I forgot (once again) to relocate from the floor to a table to prevent it from being kicked over by the featured performer who I forgot to advise not to wear a ball cap shadowing his eyes like the guy did last week 'cause…bam there goes the recorder.

Be a control freak, write it all down. No one needs to know about it except you.

Partnerships, Committees, Co-ops, & Chaos

Across the world, slam organizers have approached the task of organizing the management and production of their slams in a variety of ways. Some have chosen to fly solo. Others have formed elaborate committees complete with parliamentary procedure. Some have even developed their own full-blown nonprofit organizations with bureaucracies equal to the most cumbersome civic institution. Sometimes they get the job done. Sometimes they muck things up beyond comprehension.

Here are a few approaches that slam maestros have taken to organize their crews along with some insights on each.

A Partnership of Two or Three

You and Sammy and Sabine have been performing as a trio for years. You've learned each other's strong points, quirks, and flaws. You've fought through some nasty conflicts and survived as friends. You've bonded and you all agree that you want to step things up—go from gigging here and there to creating a weekly show.

This is a good partnership scenario. Embark on this journey with complete strangers and who knows what open manholes you may fall into, but partnering with people you trust and deal well with, even when emotions start to percolate, generally works out alright.

The keys to partnerships are respect and confidence in your copilots. Finger-pointing is out. It only consumes time and energy that are better directed toward producing a fine evening of performance poetry. You still need your checklists, but now you can divvy up the items and assist one another when a copilot stalls into a tailspin and is headed for a crash.

By Committee

Anyone who's ever sat on a committee knows the conflicts and complications that can arise. You get six opinions on how to do the most menial task, marathon arguments over what shade of blue the logo should be, complaints without recommendations, power struggles, and personality clashes. In a creative endeavor, artistic passions can intensify these conflicts and complications to a roaring extreme. Everybody's opinion becomes valid and difficult to refute diplomatically no matter how illogical or impractical it is. All the opinions may be suitable paths to the same goal, but which do you choose? And who does the choosing?

Despite these drawbacks, a hard working and harmonious committee can achieve many times more than a partnership or solo slammaster can and in half the time. In addition, collaborating with creative soul mates can often trigger synergies that enrich your vision, embellish your show, and thrill audiences. If you've got a cluster of slam lovers who are mature and confident enough to share your vision without diluting it or wrestling for control, you should strongly consider forming a committee. When your slam takes flight you'll be able to celebrate together, and that's a heck of a lot more fun than celebrating alone.

Don't give up your leadership role just because you've formed a committee. Good committees need strong leaders to balance and coordinate all the talent and ideas. Learn the strengths and weaknesses of your committee members. Don't try to remake their personalities. Tap into their talent pools and try to keep their quirks and foibles from steering the vision too far askew from the desired goal.

Cooperatives

Somewhere between committee organization and partnerships are co-operatives. Members of the cooperative are (or should be) all major players and swap roles on a regular basis. They have the ability to perform most if not all the tasks and duties required. They should have prior production experience and know exactly what to do and how to do it...they're seasoned organizers who can work with others toward a common goal.

Many cooperatives have no clear-cut leader—no one pulling rank or barking orders. Cooperative members trust one another and view themselves as a team of equals. It's like a relay race. This month Delrica and Wayne are running the show. Next month Jamie takes charge. In between Tyrone handles the website because he's a whiz at it and his brother takes over for him when he has to travel out of town for his new day job.

With a cooperative, the group can achieve more than the sum of what each individual brings to the group, because members can play off of one another's talents and ideas. As with partnerships, creative synergies can develop that make for some very interesting and unexpected discoveries and innovations.

The Three Tier Model—Combining the Best of All Worlds

For the really big show, I recommend implementing a three-tier model. I (along with all the partners who stuck by me all these years) have followed this model for all the major slam events we've created, planned, and produced. For a small event this may involve far more organizational finagling than necessary, but for festival size events it often spawns the charm that makes the magic happen.

- **Core group of four...or three...or five:** This is the partnership element. Individuals who know and respect each other, who have worked together and enjoyed it, who share a vision, who understand the strengths and weaknesses in themselves and in their partners, and who relish the interaction of pushing toward a communal goal with comrades in action form the central leadership. The Core conceptualizes the vision, sets goals, itemizes duties, and bears the responsibility for everything that has to be done.

- **The circle of dedicated doers:** Surrounding the Core are hand-picked organizers and volunteers selected to manage specific areas of planning and producing, such as marketing, transportation, accommodations, accounting, fund-raising, tournament structure, and venues. These individuals are people the Core knows will follow through and get things done. They have proven track records and often recruit equally competent people to help in their areas of focus. They direct most of their energies toward their specific tasks but can also add voice to the overall project keeping communication between various areas open and clear.

- **The big circumference of volunteers:** Over the years The Chicago Core Group responsible for staging three of the most successful national events in slam history have attracted throngs of volunteers to the big circumference by holding volunteer parties and informal gatherings designed to make things fun from the get-go. A stack of pizzas, pop, and beer; music; a little pep talk; and a poem or two enhance the camaraderie. To prevent fun tasks from becoming chores, organizers pass around slips of paper listing very specific things volunteers can sign up for and take charge of: pass out flyers for Thursdays nights bouts at the train station, pick up the St. Louis poets at the airport and drive them to their hotel, be one of the greeters at the opening ceremony downtown, carry in the sound equipment and carry it out, and so on. The big circumference volunteers bear no heavy burden. Their jobs should translate into fun—a hundred small tasks carried out by a few dozen jovial people.

The key to the three-tier method is delegating responsibilities in the right proportion to the volunteers and organizers who have stepped forward to help. Never overwhelm someone with responsibilities that turn joy into terror or drudgery. Give folks just enough duty to have a clear opportunity to succeed in a small or big capacity—the opportunity to rejoice when the curtain rises and falls knowing that they contributed to the event's success.

Help Wanted—Key Positions to Fill... If You Can

When you're the slammaster, you're ultimately responsible for everything, and that means *everything* on those lists you've created—the details and duties to ensure that your show runs smoothly, on time, and in a manner that allows you and your slam monster to breathe and grow beyond your wildest dreams.

Although you're ultimately responsible—the stanza stops with you—it doesn't mean that you have to do everything yourself. The following sections suggest areas of focus you might want to delegate to qualified members of your crew who can do them better than you:

- Marketing
- Scouting and booking talent
- Emcee-ing
- Offstage support

Marketing

You may have initiated your marketing campaign by sketching a logo, pasting up a crude flyer, running off a couple hundred copies on the sly at work, and then handing them out at poetry functions. But, when you're itching to pump up the volume and take your show to the next level, you'll need to launch a full force marketing blitz with press releases, an informative website, mass mailings, TV appearances, radio interviews, and any other marketing gimmick you can dream up. You may find yourself staring at your marketing "to do" list wishing that you'd never heard the word "slam."

Unless you're a Madison Avenue guru who finds every promotional task as gratifying as that first cup of coffee hours before the sun rises, be on the lookout for a marketing maven. The ideal candidate will have the following traits:

- An artistic flair
- The ability to write clever ad copy and kick out some catchy hype
- A pleasant telephone voice and personality
- A tenacious yet gracious follow-through demeanor that hears "yes" in the first, second, and third "no"
- A magnetism that gathers energy and allies to the cause
- A familiarity with computers, desktop publishing software, website management, networking, email, and blogging

If your slammin' by committee for a major event, name one person to be in charge of marketing, and advise that person to seek piecemeal help from a half dozen sources: someone to design logos, someone to write press releases, someone to create a website, and so on. Marketing is a big domain; the more help you have, the better.

Cyberspace

Internet capabilities for marketing and promotion are being invented and re-invented as fast as the information that flows through the cyber fibers. By the time I finish typing this sentence there will be yet another breakthrough in networking and communicating information instantly to mass audiences.

Direct mail campaigns have been replaced by email "blasts," social networking on sites like LinkedIn and Facebook, and viral marketing on blogs and sites like YouTube. Press packs are now electronic; can be distributed via websites, blogs, and email; and no longer consist of static copy and photos. Now, a press kit can be updated with relative ease and frequency to include not only the latest photos, resumes, schedules, and biographies, but also audio and video clips of last night's performances; the full text of select poems; and live links to various websites and blogs where the press can find out even more about specific artists, performances, and venues.

Find a young (or old) slam zealot who knows what's out there and what's coming and is tech savvy, and entice him or her to take control of your Internet realm or at least help with it.

Archives

Having resumes, records, and evidence of past achievements collected, assembled, and stored in good order helps when a potential sponsor, program director, or journalist asks for more information to support your claims that the Blue Bellow Slam is the greatest thing to hit your town since Venetian Gelato. All of these records and mementos are also nice to have when you meet with your old slam buddies from years gone by to reminisce about all the grand times you had.

Hobby historians might start vibrating with glee at the thought of commanding the archive post of your slam. Down the line they may see visions of holding control over some of the most important documents and video evidence in slam history—stuff that has shifted the tectonic plates of poetry posterity.

Sure, your slam might not make it into the history books, but you still need to consider what you're going to do with all the CDs, flyers, scripts, photos, and posters you'll start accumulating once your show starts rolling. And believe me, you'll start amassing quite a heap.

Several videographers in Chicago have footage of the earliest performances of the Chicago Poetry Ensemble. In 2007 a German documentary group asked if I had any early footage from the Get Me High days. I said I didn't but I might know someone who did. I referred the film group to Hugh Schwartz and Rob Van Tuyle. Clips from their archived collections appeared in the documentary, which aired across Germany and France. It also netted the Speak'Easy Ensemble (a descendant of the CPE) a sweet gig at the 2008 ABC Brecht Festival in Augsburg.

Scouting and Booking Talented Performance Poets

Obviously, even when flying solo, you can't be the one and only performer. Today, slammasters are very lucky to be able to draw from a fairly large pool of talent. Performance poets and slammers travel across the country looking for new shows to fill in their tour routes. Google terms like *slam*, *slammer*, *performance poetry*, and *spoken word,* and you'll find links to thousands of web pages with resumes of performers and ensembles you might want headlining your show.

Many performance poets have MySpace pages. Go to one of the better known slammers and check his/her list of friends, and you'll find dozens of top performers and slammers. Start with Robbie Q (www.myspace.com/theenvironment)—founding member of Chicago's Speak'Easy Ensemble.

Avidly seek out the talent in your own city, both poets and variety acts. Your goal is to develop a broad audience base that extends beyond the existing poet community. Keep a talent address book or at least a list with each performer's contact information and a one line description to jog your memory when you sit down to book performers for upcoming shows. Attend other poetry events, read reviews, and ask around to get the names and numbers of high caliber performers. Put out the word on slam bulletins and listservs that you have openings for in-town and out-of-town slammers, and they'll start calling you.

Scouting Talent

It's certainly not necessary to recruit or hire a talent scout to find your weekly or monthly performers, but it will help to let your crew know that you're open and eager to hear from them about performers and acts they see.

Be sure to check credentials before booking anyone you haven't seen and heard in action. The website might be the slickest, most professional, dynamic, and exciting one you have ever Googled, but the performance might be a step below your worst open micer. Ask for references and check with other slammasters—heed their recommendations and warnings. Giving an ambitious novice a start is commendable, but not at the expense of damaging your show's reputation.

Booking Talent

Negotiating with and scheduling talent may not be your strong suit. You might be too nice or too embarrassed to say no when they ask for a fee three times the amount the co-op has budgeted. You might be lackadaisical when it comes to dates and times and calling people back. Is there someone on your committee or in the co-op who negotiates for a living? A purchasing agent or a lawyer? Is there a volunteer who schedules every hour (every minute!) of the week with ease and joy?

You don't have to give up control over selecting the talent that graces your stage—after all, part of the reason you chose to become slammaster is because you had a specific show vision you wanted to bring to life. Keep the final word in your mouth, just get a little help when necessary.

Emcees Wanted—Charisma Required

No one individual is more important to your slam than its emcee/host—the onstage personality who will make your audience feel comfortable, bestow glamour and respect on the talent, and keep the show moving moving moving.

Whether you choose to play this role yourself or delegate the job to someone more qualified, a good emcee must exhibit the following qualities:

- **Attractiveness:** The emcee doesn't have to be a wolf whistle knockout, but he or she must have an engaging personality—full of life and passion, interesting, unique, pleasantly eccentric.

- **Charisma:** A charismatic emcee is magnetic, drawing the audience's focus and generating excitement in some mysterious way. Look for someone who can turn on the juice and fire up a crowd.

Don't believe for a second that looks don't matter on the stage. Unfortunately in our image-conscious society, they do, too much at times. The good news is that within the slam world, eccentric, individualistic appearances count more than magazine fashion. Uniqueness is celebrated. The confidence many people gain from succeeding on a slam stage through their passion and words motivates them to stop trying fit into a media mold and to celebrate, accent, and flaunt the beauty of who they are and how their creator and the universe made them. Your emcee should be a person who has a self-confident self-awareness.

- **Magnanimity:** Magnanimity (or selflessness) enables an emcee to step out of the spotlight and generously welcome others into it. Magnanimous people generally are self-fulfilled; they're happy with their lives and want to celebrate other people's joy.

- **Audience Sensitivity:** Engaging emcees have a sixth sense as to what the audience is thinking and feeling. They make just the right quip, comment, or introduction to let the audience know they have a representative onstage—someone who's going to deliver on par or better to the audience's expectations.

- **Flexibility:** The ability to switch directions in reaction to the audience response or lack thereof is essential. If in the first ten minutes of a three hour show, the emcee notices that no one laughed at the dirty limericks that were tossed to the crowd, he might have to shift gears and clean up the act.

As a result of slam's worldwide success and the media attention accompanying it, many slammers and emcees have adopted stereotypes that work counter to their individuality. It's one of the consequences of success. If you're striking a pose, donning a hat, delivering a rhyme scheme, or gesturing in a way that belies your true self, you might ask yourself why? Being more you and less of somebody else could trigger a style that catapults you high above the herd that's merely following the current spoken word fashions.

- **Coolness:** The ability to think quickly under pressure without becoming flustered enables the emcee to stay the course when the show falters. Multitasking skills are a must for the emcee, who many times is required to not only introduce poets, but cue them, adjust the sound and lights, and deal with questions from reporters and audience members. You don't want your emcee forcing a smile onstage and then baring fangs to back tables when the pressure's on.

- **Talent:** Emcees are performers, too, so they should be as (or almost as) comfortable, engaging, and entertaining onstage as the performers they introduce. Many times they'll have to fill in for a guest poet who got lost in an unfamiliar city or while an inexperienced open mic poet shuffles through his papers to find the paper wadded poem he wants to read. Dead air is bad air on the stage.

- **Preparedness:** A well-stocked repertoire of performance material can help bail out an emcee when the show starts to sag.

If you're watching your slam bomb and hearing your brain chattering, "Why doesn't Emcee Julio do something?" or "Why can't Julio shut up and get on to the next poet?" maybe it's time to issue an emcee pink slip.

- **Resourcefulness:** A good emcee does what's required to make the show run smoothly regardless of the tasks required. If the mic needs adjusting, the emcee does it on the spot instead of calling the sound tech or slammaster.

- **Generosity:** A good emcee is generous to the poets and patrons, yet savvy enough not to be bowled over by hecklers or arrogant performers.

- **Dedication:** The right emcee understands your vision of the slam and wants to bring it to life.

Auditioning Emcees

Before turning the reins over to a prospective emcee, check her out in person and in action. Attend one of her performances. Ask her to come to your show and host a portion of the open mic or referee the slam competition. Assess how she interacts with the audience and uses the traits described above. When you find a candidate or two, talk with them casually and give them some rope to let the inner workings of their personalities unravel. Ask them a few questions:

- What do you think about different styles of poetry?

- What do you think about slam poetry?

- What are your ambitions?

- Did you ever punch a poet in the nose?

If they think poetry should remain locked and chained in the ivory towers and that slam poets should be institutionalized or if their lifelong ambition is to write obituaries, you'll want to continue your search. However, if your candidate did well onstage, thinks that slam has a grand future as a performance art, loves the stage but doesn't hog the light, and thanked you for the chance to help, you may have found the perfect match to fire up your show. Just make sure your personalities click and the person understands and supports your vision.

Relief Pitchers—Cohosts Need Charisma, Too

Many slams divide the duties of hosting and emceeing between members of their crew. At some slams, the slammaster acts as both host and emcee, but has a crew member referee the competition. At others, the slammaster might act as host for the first portion of the show meeting/greeting/seating people, and then take the stage only to introduce the emcee who warms up the crowd and steers the show to its conclusion. However you set up your show, you should consider having two or more personalities act as host, cohost, and emcee, even if only on a part-time basis.

> The terms *emcee, slam host*, and *slammaster* are often used interchangeably, because the slammaster often does the duties of all three. The emcee is the onstage personality introducing the acts. The host is the person in charge of organizing all the details of a particular event and greeting the clientele and performers. The slammaster is the organizer responsible for all the events of a particular slam venue and who has a direct relationship with and responsibility to PSI.

Once you line up a dynamite emcee, be on the lookout for backups or build sub-emcees into the ritual of your show by trying out different personalities in different positions. You might enlist a main emcee to be responsible for the overall direction of the show and a co-emcee (or cohost) to referee the slam competition or introduce guest performers. Sometimes the emcee role is too important to leave to a single person; make sure you have a couple fine options in the bullpen in case the starter calls in sick, gets hurt, or just doesn't show.

Different personalities draw different fans and can help expand your audience base. The host might be warm and welcoming, making reticent patrons feel at home, whereas the emcee has an edgy sense of humor that appeals to the more daring, experienced clientele. Different personalities add variety to the overall slam experience. They also help promote your show through casual word-of-mouth advertising. "Hey everybody! Come by the Goose Neck Slam next week. I'm hosting it!" It also trains more people and creates more leaders for the movement in general and could possibly lead to more shows in your town.

Offstage Support

Patrons leave your show replaying the performances in their minds. That's what they came for—to escape the mundane and revel in the visions and re-creations of the onstage spectacle. However, much of the work that goes into making any show a success goes on offstage, and people generally don't remember it unless something goes wrong. If the lighting cast faces in shadows, if the sound system emitted buzzes and cracks, if Wammo's fan club had to wait in line for a half hour while the ticket taker looked for change, Wammo's mother will remember *that* above anything else, and will probably mention it to every Tom, Deedee, and Harriet for the next six weeks. To make sure no crisis offstage undermines your show's onstage integrity, assemble a good crew to handle the "minor" details, as explained in the following sections.

Sound and Light Technicians

Chapter 9 covers what you need to know about managing a sound system and illuminating your stage. In your initial vision, you saw yourself acting as host and perhaps as the show's emcee. But now after you've staged a few events playing all these roles and doing everything else, you've discovered that if you're adjusting the lights and fiddling with the sound system, you're missing the beauty of the banquet you've brought into being. It's like having a dinner party and spending the entire evening in the kitchen.

Every slam family has one gifted consumer electronics whiz who loves playing with the stereo and adding mood lighting to his bedroom. If this electro-wizard isn't too far out there (strobe lights, echo chambers), give the whiz a shot at managing the technical details of your show.

Door Person

An honest, reliable, and charming, or at least interesting (as in eccentric) door person is a must, especially for shows just starting out. Nightclubs and other over twenty-one establishments sometimes insist on having their own door person checking IDs and collecting the cover charge. That saves you the expense of hiring someone, but it gives you no control over the money or how the patrons are greeted. Be sure you're comfortable with the door person, and if you have reservations about the person, express them to the owner or manager in a diplomatic way.

> An experienced door person can often handle several additional tasks: the sign-up sheets, passing out flyers, checking the guest list, and ordering pizzas for the after-show pig out.

Scorekeepers / Timers

If you're not too concerned with accuracy, assign audience members to these positions. Hand them a digital wristwatch that bleeps out the seconds, a pen, and a pad of paper. If the slam is serious, like a competition to determine who goes on tour with Viggo Mortenson, you might want to buy some stopwatches and calculators and appoint someone in your crew to manage these tasks. Whomever you use as scorekeepers and timers, give them a brief lesson on their duties and instruct the emcee to watch over them and bail them out when they screw up, because they will screw up, they always do...at least once. Hey, that's part of the show, too.

Merchandise Sellers

The role of merchant is a dedicated job that should be delegated only to a loyal assistant or trustworthy volunteer. It involves record keeping, money handling, pitching, and schmoozing. If you can put a couple people on this task, do it. Sitting alone at a table far back from where the action's happening can get lonely and boring, and who's watching the money when your merchandise person needs relief?

Judges

Usually slam judges are selected from the audience, but sometimes they're recruited ahead of time either to add a higher level of legitimacy to the competition or, in the case of slams just starting out, to be sure someone is on hand to do the job. Look back to Chapter 3 to review how to make judge selection part of the show, part of the ritual, and enhance the entertainment value of the night.

In-House Ensembles

You learned earlier that the Chicago Poetry Ensemble was vital to the initial success of the Uptown Poetry Slam at the Green Mill. They injected pizzazz, spectacle, and daring poetics into the first shows. They also doubled up on production tasks ranging from covering the door to acting as last minute ringers in the open mic and competition.

It's not unusual for shoestring theater and entertainment operations to ask their performers to help with the tech. Everyone pitches in serving the cause in a variety of capacities. And this is the greatest attribute of, and reason for having, an in-house ensemble. They're an insurance policy to cover those eleventh hour flubs and loopholes as well as serving as a surefire staple of proven entertainment.

Trustworthy and Reliable Assistants

When you're focused on crafting a show that packs a wallop, it's easy to overlook the minor details, and there are zillions of them—from purchasing markers and scorecards to making sure the mailing lists get circulated. A dedicated *assistant* show manager or slammaster can be a great relief, ensuring that attention gets paid to every aspect of the show. Every small detail that's polished and nailed in place helps push your slam to greater heights. The following list describes the duties that you can expect a competent assistant to handle before, during, and after a show:

- **Setup:** Arrange the furniture and set up the stage (mic in place, lights working, sound system okay). Stack and set out flyers announcing future events. Seat people and answer questions. Check to be sure the feature performers have arrived or are on their way.

- **During the Show:** Get open micers lined up and on the mark. Provide hospitality to guest performers. Monitor sound and lights. Cue the emcee about announcements and what's coming next. Keep track of contact information. Handle prizes.

- **Afterward:** Put away the furniture where the venue owner wants it. Help clean up, if the venue is one where this is required. Help put away any stuff you came with, including markers, index cards, mailing list, lights. Make sure the performers aren't pacing the parking lot looking for jumper cables. Direct everyone to the after-show party place.

If you remember anything, remember...

- Creating and staging a show by yourself may be rewarding, but it can become too demanding for any single person.

- Partnerships, committees, and co-ops serve three basic purposes: to share responsibility, to distribute the workload, and to foster synergies that energize the show.

- For larger shows, consider following the Three Tier Model consisting of a Core Group, Dedicated Doers, and a Circumference of Volunteers.

- When delegating, give special focus to the following four areas: marketing, talent, emcees, and offstage support.

- Make sure your show's emcee has a personality that clicks with yours, understands and supports your vision for the show, and has all the qualities of an outstanding host and performer.

- An in-house ensemble is a valuable addition to any show, providing background music and musical accompaniment, filling in gaps in the show, and acting as ringers when poets don't show up.

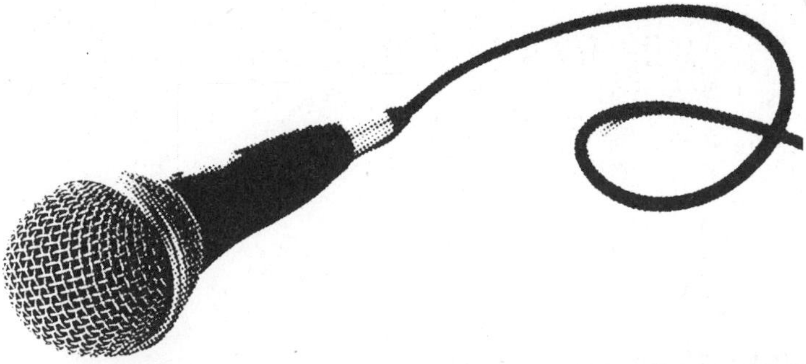

NEXT UP!

Know What You're Promoting

Form Follows Function—Marketing Materials

Branding Logo

Cheap, but Effective: Flyers and Postcards

Not as Cheap, but Very Effective: Posters

Generating Feature Stories, Interviews, and Media Attention

Step 1: Write a Press Release

Step 2: Send the Press Release

Step 3: Call 'Em

Work Your Angle

Press the Airwaves

More Methods for Getting the Word Out

Free Listings

Managing Mailing (and Emailing) Lists

Paid Ads

Establishing a Web Presence

Blog

Launch a Website

Populate Your Website or Blog with Content

Promote Your Website or Blog

Explore Social Networks

Share Podcasts of Show Highlights

Post Video Clips on YouTube

Never Underestimate Word of Mouth

Press the Flesh

Cool Calls

How Much Promoting... and to Whom?

How Many People Do You Need to Reach?

Motivating Yourself with Deadlines

The Push

If you remember anything, remember...

11

GETTING THE WORD OUT: PUBLICIZING YOUR SHOW

You've scratched your vision into a plan. You've assembled your crew and put them to work implementing it. You've lit the room, built the stage, and switched on the amplification. And now you're ready to wow an eager audience...Audience?! Oops! You forgot the audience?!

You can have the World Series of slams, but if you don't push to promote it, your lineup of slam champions will be performing to a sea of empty seats. And nobody wants that.

It's time to gear up and pound the pavement, agitate the airwaves, and squeal from the rooftops to let anybody and everybody know what they'll miss if they don't shake off the inertia and climb onboard your slam express. Like a Madison Avenue marketing mogul, you'll need to persuade the most firmly rooted of couch potatoes that the stay-at-home video movies and microwave popcorn take second place to your show's itinerary.

This chapter highlights basic tools and strategies that will help the novice show maker get the word out. As your slam-making reputation grows, you'll need to add more and more tools and strategies to your box of promo magic, maybe even hire an agency to promote next year's grand slam festival, but for now, the fundamentals described in this chapter should get the marketing rock rolling.

Know What You're Promoting

The nature of your show, its essence, defines and drives the strategy you employ to promote it. And the best way to find that strategy's focus is to come up with a succinct understanding of what you have to offer. Is your show comedic or dramatic, or both? Is star power in the lineup? Are you planning a royal gimmick to open and close the show... maybe drag queen slammers roller-skating between the tables or poets composing take-home limericks for audience members as they file out the door?

How your slam is presented in the marketing materials you develop can make or break your advertising efforts. An all-ages pop poetry concert requires poster art that would doom a senior citizen open mic. A portrait of Willy Shakespeare on a flyer for your Death Jam Poetry Armageddon is not going to motivate the mosh pit crowd to sharpen up their spiked bracelets and start dancing to sonnets.

Dynamic shows are not one-note sambas. They're filled with surprises and compelling performances—packed with variety. The Sunday night slam at the Green Mill has been described as a circus, a church, a town meeting, and a free-for-all. That's great as a general marketing description, but it doesn't have the necessary focus to pitch individual events.

There's a blurry distinction between *marketing* and *promotional* activities and tools. The overlap makes them seem the same, but I'm told there's a difference. For this discussion *marketing* refers to the work done and tools created to brand your show in general. *Promotion* refers to the activities and tools employed to fill the seats at a particular event.

Let's say you've lined up Ralphie, the local shock jock whom everybody knows by first name and recognizes on sight, to host your first all-city slam tournament. Ralphie's your selling point. Your goal as marketing maven is to make his name and face synonymous with the event by tattooing Ralphie on all your marketing tools and eventually on the brain cells of John Q. Public. Or maybe your show features acrobatic poets versifying through backflips and human pyramids; if so, pitch that as your main attraction. Create an image of bodies and words cart wheeling across the stage, and then drill that image into the hearts and minds of your prospective audience.

> If you do hire some backflipping poets, you might want to look into some event insurance or check with the venue to be sure it has liability coverage. It's one thing to get smacked by a metaphor, but quite another to be flattened by a flipper...or a lawsuit.

You have dozens of angles to consider when trying to find the hot selling points for an event. Asking yourself the following questions can help zero in on how to make the most of your marketing time and materials.

- Is your slam brand-new? Is it the longest running slam in town?
- Does it explore a specific theme or showcase a particular style? The Dead Poet Revival? The Food Fight Slam?
- Will your special guests appeal to a certain demographic? Are they controversial? Have they just released a new publication?
- Does your slam feature music? Costumes? Ensemble work? Rivalries between local poet heroes?
- What's the lowdown on the performers? Any big media dandies?

Discover your show's strongest selling points and use them to guide you as you prepare your marketing materials.

Form Follows Function—Marketing Materials

A plethora of marketing materials and media are available for promoting slams; you just need to choose the forms that will hit your target audience and effectively communicate your show's top selling points. If your slam vision is a Punch and Judy Puppet Poetry Hour at the local library, special invitations sent to grade school teachers accompanied by colorful posters to hang in the halls is going to do more than a mass mailing to your nightclub regulars. A midnight Raise the Dead Slam might demand a psychedelic print ad in the *Weed* newsletter. A public radio announcement might not be the best choice for an ASL (American Sign Language) open mic for the hearing impaired. The following sections describe marketing/promotional tools you'll need to create for any type of slam you choose to stage.

Branding Logo

"Bongo the Bootmaker." "Trolley Times." "Mouth of America." Everything has a brand name these days and a logo to go with it. And because you're competing in a marketplace filled with entertainment and arts options galore, it'll help if you have one, too. I came up with a catchy name, "Slam Poetry," and look what happened. A captivating name pins a memorable mental image on the public's forehead, making it nearly impossible for people to keep from thinking about it every time they look into their memory's mirror.

One way to invent a catchy name is to think of words and phrases that communicate vital information about your event:

Location: *Uptown Poetry Slam* or *Horseshoe Bend Poetry Slampede*

Day, Date, or Time: *Blue Monday Poetry Hour* or *Hump Day Poetry Battle*

Theme: *Fat Tuesday Celebration of the Seven Deadly Sins* or *Head to Head Haiku*

Always try to insert a sliver of mystery into the name to get folks curious about what's up and spur them to make an effort to find out more by reading the fine print or asking the counter kid "What's up?" For example:

Slam Dunk Poetry Day. "What the heck is that? Poets stuffing words through hoops?"

Poetry Hot Dog Stand. "Are the poets serving fries wrapped in poetic napkins?"

Louder than a Bomb. "Is that another cheesy war flick? Kids reading poetry! About blowing things up?"

After you have a name, transform it into a show logo by blowing up the letters BIG and Clever in an EYECatchy font, or by strong-arming a design student in love with slammin' and giving her the poetic license to ink out an image to enhance the name. Your logo needs to visually SHOUT the news of your event from flyers, posters, websites, letterheads, T-shirts, and an assortment of other marketing materials you haven't even conjured up yet.

Go to www.poetryslam.com/nps/history.htm and take a gander at the different logos host cities have designed for the annual NPS (National Poetry Slam) events.

Cheap, but Effective: Flyers and Postcards

Throughout your life, you've probably seen thousands of flyers, postcards, and handbills. They're pasted on walls, tacked to bulletin boards, stuffed into mailboxes, and buried under mounds of clutter. Some you don't notice at all. Some you pick up and throw away. Some you keep in your pocket or hang on the fridge for months. Why do you hold on to a particular flyer?

Like all effective advertisements, eye-catching artwork and brain-gripping words are key, but the design probably carries with it essential information you can't forget to include no matter how sassy and seductive the artwork looks:

- Date of the event
- Branding logo
- Venue address (and directions if the show is at a remote site)
- A description of the show (guest performers and what's happening, the selling points)
- Starting time
- Cover charge or ticket price
- A phone number to call for more information

The battle for attention on the flyer walls is intense. The shapes and sizes of postings are constantly evolving. When someone comes up with a new color combination (shape or size) that stands out, everyone copies it. The new and effective style soon becomes commonplace until the next new idea jumps off the wall. Standard paper sizes and economics govern choices but practicality is often sacrificed for an extraordinary design that the promoter is convinced will attract attention and fill seats.

Postcards must be rectangular; at least 3.5-by-5 inches and .007 inch thick; and no larger than 4.25-by-6 inches and .016 inch thick to qualify for the lower postcard rate. Flyers and handbills range in size from 8.5-by-11 inches to business card size. It might be ingenious to pass out circular flyers, but they could also cost a chunk of change to produce. You make the call. Remember that golden rule of advertising: What would *stop you* and say, "Look at me?"

Not as Cheap, but Very Effective: Posters

Quality posters give your show an air of success. They are larger and pricier than flyers, but people notice them. They place your show on a level above the rookie, home-brew status. Coffee shops, storefronts, taverns, restaurants, libraries, and cultural centers often allow promoters to display large posters in their windows and on their bulletin boards.

The key to postering is to approach the owners and managers with humility and grace. If you're out there beating the pavement, they might admire your dedication and hard work. In most cases, they will eagerly support your efforts to add something valuable to the community. If they know nothing about you, visit them and make their acquaintance. Strike a deal to put their menu in your newsletter or plan a postshow party at their bar. Use good manners. Ask before you put something up, don't cover up other people's stuff, and bring your own tape and pushpins.

Generating Feature Stories, Interviews, and Media Attention

Contrary to popular belief, news cameras and journalists don't possess some innate skill that allows them to find the Next Big Thing. They need to be coaxed and reminded of it constantly. Part of your job as slammaster/show maker is to alert them to the existence of your slam and sell them on its dynamics.

> One of the best marketing tools of all time is a *great review.* People follow what the "experts" say, and when it comes to slam, the critics are the "experts." If they praise your show, the masses will flock to it. If they pan it, the masses will scamper away. And when a radio or newspaper critic reports that your show is "dazzling," incorporate that praise into your marketing materials.

Why do you want the press to know about and possibly attend your show? Because they produce pictures and copy that a lot of people see—a lot more people than are going to pick up a flyer or scrutinize a poster. Articles, pictures, and interviews also build your street cred and supply you with ready made (at no cost to you) materials to use and reuse for promoting future events.

The formula for press attention is simple: Write a press release, send it out, and follow up with a phone call. The following sections provide the details.

Step 1: Write a Press Release

If you're a busy reporter on deadline with fifty-two press releases piled on your desk and a feature story to cook up in ten minutes, what would cause *you* to pull out one from the pile and not the others? Probably something eye-catching, professional, and direct. Journalists are busy people, so plenty of white space between the bullets and paragraphs makes for fast reading. They want to know immediately the who, what, and when—mixed with something that's smart and convincing, showing them that your event is newsworthy and worth the public's time to experience and the journalist's reputation to write about.

Standard formats govern the design and layout of press releases. Consult a friend in the media biz or call the features editor of the *Town News* and ask them to send you a few examples. If they're busy, go on a fact-finding mission between the aisles of the city library or to the journalism department of your local university. Surf the Internet to find samples, guidelines, and services regarding press releases.

Incorporate the essential information you've included on your flyers and postcards (see above) into a one-page presentation and dress it up a bit by embellishing your selling points. But not too much! Never write a press release that's longer than a single page—the editors and reporters won't read it. Give them a spicy good taste, not a whole meal. If they want more information, they'll call you. So be sure to include in **bold print** your full contact information at the top of the page, where it's easy to find at a glance.

And proofread it carefully (twice) before sending it out. Ask a friend or relative, preferably someone who's fairly literate, to read it over, as well. Nothing exposes an amateur more surely than misspellings and careless syntax, especially when that somebody is supposedly a big shot slammaster.

Step 2: Send the Press Release

The obvious next step after writing your press release is to send it out. The most difficult aspect of this is to find who to send it to and when. Send it too early (months before your event) and it'll end up at the bottom of a pile or in the trash because it's not relevant to the features editor at that moment in time. Check with someone in the news biz to see what's appropriate to local publications—a rule of thumb is two or three weeks before a performance. If you're sending the press release to a monthly magazine, they might need a little more lead time.

If you're managing an ongoing slam, don't expect the media to write stories about it every week. If they cover it four times a year you're doing great. That doesn't mean you should stop pitching them whenever there's something special coming up. Keep them informed. It shows that your slam is alive and thriving whether they write about it or not.

Use the Internet to hunt down publications in your area. A simple search like "newspaper DeKalb Illinois" will cover a lot of ground. Specialty publications such as newsletters for libraries or literary institutions may require a more arduous hunt. Check newspaper and magazine websites for fax numbers, mailing addresses, and the personal email contact info for the department or editor you want to target, or call the office to obtain the information. Find the names and contact info for specific reporters covering poetry events and send your press release directly to them.

Step 3: Call 'Em

You don't want to be a nuisance, but a week or so after you've sent the release, call the newspaper office and ask them if they received it. Invite them to come to your event and offer to provide them with additional information and photos. The worse they can do is say "not interested." The best they can do is come to the show, enjoy your performance, and generate press about you and the show. The venue owner will be happy and appreciative of the media attention and free PR. The journalist will be happy because she got a cool story. So don't forget the follow-up call.

Work Your Angle

Just as every city poet needs a city poem, every journalist needs an angle. How should a reporter from the *Blandsville Bugle* write about a slam when he's usually writing up the minutes from the City Council meeting on street cleaning? He has to make his story relevant to his audience, put an intriguing spin on it.

In your press release, or in your phone conversation with the reporter, you should think about an angle he could take in his story. If he's any good, he'll figure this out for himself, but it never hurts to point the reporter in the desired direction, the selling points.

Slam's international reputation is one of the main selling points for novice slammasters to exploit. Very few reporters would balk at writing a feature article about a world-renowned circus coming to town, even a poetry circus called slam.

Press the Airwaves

When you're looking for press coverage, don't lock your focus on the printed word; send your press release to radio and TV stations, as well. Consider including an audio recording (for radio stations) or a video clip (for TV stations).

Advertising on television is probably the most effective marketing tool on the planet. Manufacturers use it to peddle their products and services, politicians use it to promote their platforms, and nonprofits use it to attract new members and solicit contributions. Unfortunately, it's not cheap; even a brief, local, TV spot comes in at anywhere from $350 to $50,000!

Radio is often a better vehicle for a slammaster. It's verbal, relatively affordable, and it typically plays to the target audience—people who like to listen to music, experience the community's night life, and take a chance on new forms of entertainment, including poetry slams.

Paying for TV ads might be out of your reach, but persuading local TV news and arts programming to cover it is not—especially when it's related to a major event such as a regional or national slam. Call the producers and pitch them an exciting image and angle, and there's a good chance they'll show up with camera crew in tow. TV is a hungry beast that needs constant feeding. Feed the beast.

More Methods for Getting the Word Out

Enlisting the power of the news media to spread the word that the slam circus is coming to town is without a doubt one of the most effective ways to pass the word around, but it's certainly not the only one. You can take matters into your own hands and start a grass roots marketing blitz that could be highly effective. In the following sections, I describe some additional options that have worked well for me and other slammers.

Free Listings

Most daily and weekly entertainment and arts sections have free listings. They look like classified ads. You type up the details of your event and email them to the listings editor on or before the deadline, and the editor prints it under an appropriate heading free of charge.

For high profile nonprofit performances, you may be able to persuade local radio stations to run a public service announcement (PSA) about your event. Broadcasting laws require them to run a certain number of these each week. You'll have to provide them a ready-for-air recording of the announcement and be content with it airing when they find time for it.

The Internet has many options for no-cost advertising through MySpace and Facebook pages and other networking services. Take advantage of any and all of these if you can, and don't forget to attach your logo to the announcements whenever possible. (For more about marketing and promoting your slam on the Web, check out "Establishing a Web Presence," later in this chapter.)

Managing Mailing (and Emailing) Lists

Begin developing a mailing list today. Start with your personal address book. Get some user-friendly software and type in all the names and numbers you know. (In a pinch, you can always use a standard spreadsheet program such as Microsoft Excel.)

- Plan to have a mailing list sign-up sheet at every event, and make sure it gets passed around and returned to you at the end of the night.
- Take the list home and add the names to your database.
- Send out simple email messages informing everyone of your events.
- Create a monthly newsletter to inform your fans of long-range plans, fun gossip, and how they can get more deeply involved in your slam and the slam family.
- Update your list regularly by removing invalid addresses and records of people requesting to be removed from the list.

If you do too much mass emailing, your online service or Internet service provider might suspect you of spamming and put you on probation or cancel your account altogether. Read your provider's rules on spam before you start emailing with wild abandon.

Some slam fans don't have computers or email accounts (or just don't want to hand out their email addresses). In such cases, you might need to mail hardcopy flyers to them. Snail mail costs a little more (a hundred flyers at forty-four cents a piece equals forty-four bucks) but if it helps build a loyal fan base, it's worth it.

When I started the Get Me High show in 1984, I had a snail list of fifty names I borrowed from my friend and partner Ron Gillette. Every week I religiously mailed out flyers to the names on the list, which grew to over 500 by the end of 1985. I figured that if only one out five on the list attended a show now and then it was well worth the time and expense I put into it.

Paid Ads

Big time promoters with deep pockets take out full-page color ads in the major dailies, and thousands of readers see them. What an enviable luxury! If your pockets aren't so deep, consider some alternatives. In most midsize cities, at least three or four neighborhood or trade papers are published daily or weekly. Major metropolitan areas have many more than that. Choose a paper that fits your audience and budget, take out an ad, and see what happens.

Call the local newspaper's classified ads department and ask about *remnant ads*. Frequently, newspapers can't sell enough ads to cover an entire page, so they have blank spots that they usually use to post a filler like "Your Ad Could Be Here." It's like flying standby; if they have room for your ad at the last minute, they plug it in an open spot—and you pay a lot less than the going rate. Unfortunately, you can't count on having your ad posted on a particular day.

Establishing a Web Presence

The Internet has been essential to the growth of the slam movement. Through chat rooms, personal websites, blogs, venue home pages, social networking sites (such as MySpace and Facebook), and video sharing sites including YouTube, word about slam and poetry performance has spread far and wide.

Just about everybody who stages and promotes any type of show eventually finds themselves in front of a computer screen, and just about every computer screen is hooked up to the net. So, get wired and start establishing a presence on the Web. Here's why:

- **It's fast.** You don't have to send out a press release and wait for the media to pick it up... if they ever do. You *are* the press. In a matter of a few hours (at most), you can have a blog or website up and running and start posting information about your venue and your show, including photos and video clips, creating a multimedia marketing kiosk for all to see.

- **It's effective.** Hordes of people prowl the Web for information. Establishing a presence on the Web gives you a shot at reaching these people when they Google "slam poetry" along with the name of your town or Google the name of performers you mention on your site. In addition, if you can get other performers, organizations, and venues to link to your site, you can catch the attention of even more eyeballs. This not only helps you attract the biggest fans, but it also attracts the top talent.

- **It's relatively inexpensive.** Several services allow you to set up a website or blog for free in a matter of minutes. You can post video clips to YouTube for the time it takes to upload the clip. Even if you want to create a custom website or blog with your own domain name (such as HamSlamRocks.com), you can do it for less than a hundred bucks a year.

- **It's hot, it's hip**. A lot, and I do mean a *lot,* of poetry fans (and poets) lurk around online. Whether they're updating their own sites, chatting in chat rooms or in online poetry forums, or checking scores from the latest bout at Nationals, anyone who's interested in what's happening in the world of poetry is online. You can connect with these people, attract new patrons, communicate with your core clientele, reach out to new talent, and establish a stronger presence as the place to be.

In the following sections, I introduce you to a few of the many ways you can begin to establish a presence on the Web, using it to market your slam and promote specific events.

Blog

One of the easiest and quickest ways to start establishing a presence on the Web is to create your own blog. A *blog* is an online journal of sorts where you can post about what's going on in your life, what you're thinking, and anything else imaginable. Posting an entry is as simple as typing into a form and then clicking a button. The blog platform (software) takes care of the rest, formatting your entry and placing it on your blog.

Visitors to your blog can add comments to your post. This makes the blog infinitely more interactive than a standard website. If you post plenty of relevant and interesting content, you'll soon discover a community growing around your blog—a community that has the potential of attracting new patrons.

The blogging platform allows you to completely change the appearance of your blog simply by choosing a different *design template.* The template controls the appearance of everything on your blog, including the titles you assign your entries, each entry's text, the blog's background colors and design, and the way everything is positioned on the blog.

In the companion book on becoming a slam poet, I point out that blogs are a great place for poets to post their poetry and keep fans informed of upcoming performances. Blogs are just as great for slammasters to promote their slams.

One of the coolest features of a blog is that it enables you to create static *pages* as well as regular *posts*. You can create a page of photos showing what the venue looks like, another page of photos of poets who've performed at your slam, a calendar of upcoming shows and events, a page of testimonials from patrons and performers, a page for press releases and press clippings, a separate page for your bio, a page where people can sign up to receive your newsletter, and more. Through the posting feature, you can post your thoughts and insights on upcoming shows, describe anything interesting that happened at past shows, and even engage patrons and poets in creative brainstorming sessions about plans for upcoming shows and events. Posts generally appear on the opening page of your blog in reverse chronological order (most recent post first).

Several services on the Web provide free blogging, including the following:

- WordPress at wordpress.com
- Blogger at www.blogger.com
- Yahoo! 360° at 360.yahoo.com

The only drawback to using one of these free services is that they don't provide you with your own domain name, such as YourName.com. In most cases, you assign a name that's attached to the service's domain. So your domain would be something more along the lines of YourName.blogger.com. In addition, some services might display ads on your page, consuming space and distracting visitors from the important stuff. For more control, you're better off creating an independent blog using a commercial hosting service.

One of the great features about blogs is that the more entries you post and the more comments that visitors post in response to your entries, the more attractive your blog becomes to search engines (such as Google, Yahoo!, and MSN). Be sure to post entries at least twice a week and encourage visitors to post comments. The more interesting and interactive you can make your blog, the more popular it will become.

Launch a Website

If you're not going to post new content regularly (at least ever week or so), having a blog is probably not the best option for you. If you don't post regularly, visitors quickly lose interest and wander off to more dynamic blogs. In your case, a website might be the better solution. You can post a Welcome page that provides a description of your slam and includes links to other pages, such as a venue page, a calendar of upcoming shows and events, your bio, and maybe a page where people can email you for more information or to sign up to be included on your mailing list, and then simply update your calendar whenever necessary.

Although a website tends to be a little more difficult to set up and maintain than a blog, most hosting services provide templates and tools to simplify the process. At Bluehost.com, for example, you can register a domain name and have the service host your website for you for about $80 per year. Bluehost provides tools that enable you to create and design web pages right online.

Several services also allow you to create a website for free, assuming you need a site that's pretty small and basic and you don't want your own unique domain name:

- Yahoo! GeoCities at geocities.yahoo.com
- Weebly at www.weebly.com
- Homestead at www.homestead.com

Populate Your Website or Blog with Content

Although the process of setting up a blog or website can be somewhat daunting, especially if you're not the resident geek, populating it with content can also be a challenge. Start with material you already have—a description of your slam (or how you envision it), photos of the venue, press releases you've written, your logo, flyers or posters, and perhaps press clippings. Don't worry about packing your site chock full just yet. You can expand it over time as you collect more material.

Shortly after launching your site, visit it yourself to make sure it looks as good as it did when you created it and to check that all the links work. Fix any problems immediately; otherwise, visitors might become so frustrated trying to navigate the site that they never get to the good stuff.

> Think carefully about your site's background and overall design. Remember that you want to brand your slam, so give it a look that's consistent with your slam vision and with all of your other marketing materials. If everything else has a Goth edge to it and you use a bright background covered with daisies, your site won't reinforce the image you're trying to establish.

You don't need to rely solely on yourself to populate your website or blog with content. In fact, you'll probably do better by encouraging other people (patrons, poets, volunteers) to contribute. Building your website or blog can become a community effort that generates excitement and buzz and makes people feel that they belong to something worthwhile. Your fellow contributors will have a vested interest in your slam's success.

Promote Your Website or Blog

Just as you must get the word out about your slam, you need to spread the word about your site. Write a press release announcing your site, so patrons and poets can check it out. Include your website or blog address on ALL of your promotional materials, as well—flyers, posters, postcards, press releases, whatever. Add it to all your email correspondence, paint it on the side of your car, airbrush it on your T-shirts, tattoo it on your forehead. Okay, I'm getting a little carried away, but you get the idea—promote your website or blog, so it can promote your slam.

If you know others in the community who have websites or blogs (including the owner of the venue where you stage your slams, the local library, poets, patrons, your parents, and so on), ask them to include a link on their sites that points to yours. In addition, some search sites, such as Yahoo!, allow users to recommend sites to be included in their database. (Check the bottom of the opening Yahoo! page for a link that pulls up a page telling you what to do.) By adding your site's address to the database, it's more likely that a link for your site will pop up when someone searches for "slam poetry" followed by your town's name or some other words or phrases that are prominent on and unique to your site.

> Be generous. If the venue owner links to your site, add a link to the venue's site. If you've had outstanding performers grace your stage, add links to their sites. As others experience your generosity, they will begin to return the favors and help promote your site and your slam.

Explore Social Networks

Social networks enable you to rub elbows with thousands of people who share your interest in slam poetry. Two of the more popular online hangouts are MySpace (at MySpace.com) and Facebook (at

Facebook.com). You may also want to check out LinkedIn (at, you guessed it, LinkedIn.com).

At these social networking sites, you simply register for an account and then create your own "space" where you can post information about yourself, messages that you want to share with others, photos, video clips, and so on.

Once you've set up your own area on the social networking site, you can invite other members to be your "friends," which usually means that they can post messages to your area and you can post to theirs.

To find fellow slam aficionados on MySpace, go to MySpace.com, click inside the Search box in the upper right corner of the opening page, type **slam poetry**, click the down arrow next to Web, click MySpace, and click Search. Last I checked, there were about 15,000 MySpace pages that included the term "slam poetry."

Don't forget to use your Facebook and MySpace accounts to drive traffic to your website or blog.

Share Podcasts of Show Highlights

If you record your shows or one or more of your performers recorded their performance, ask the person for permission to add a podcast of their performance to your site. This enables visitors to listen in on a typical show and sample what they're missing out on. Just make sure the recording is of high enough quality, the performance is top notch, and you can hear a pretty good crowd roar its approval at the end.

1. Convert the audio clips into a digital format (such as MP3), if they're not already digital.

2. Upload the audio files to a podcast hosting service. If you

already have a hosting service, follow their instructions. You can access the following free podcast hosting services: www.ourmedia.org, www.blogger.com, or www.feedburner.com to name a few.

3. Add links to your website or blog that point to the location of your podcasts.

Post Video Clips on YouTube

Google's YouTube is a free service that enables anyone with a video recording device and a little know-how to post video clips that are instantly accessible to a potential audience of hundreds of millions of people.

To see how it's done, visit YouTube at YouTube.com and search for "slam poet." You'll find thousands of video clips of slam poets performing onstage and off. (Before you post clips of other performance poets, make sure you have their permission to do so, preferably in writing.)

When you're ready to post a video clip on YouTube, simply visit the website, click the Upload button, and follow the on-screen instructions. (You have to be a registered YouTube user to post your own video clips.)

> After you post a video clip on YouTube, be sure to go back to your website or blog and add a link to one of your posts or pages that points to your video.

Never Underestimate Word of Mouth

You can spend thousands of dollars on the slickest, glossiest, and most eye-popping ad materials a sugar-mommy can buy and then raise the curtain on your big night only to find *nobody* in the audience! (All of mama's money down the drain.) On the other hand, Louie down the street who's been cooking up a night of erotica every third Friday for the past three years doesn't bother printing up flyers or making phone

Rangeview Library District
Anythink Perl Mack
303 428-3576
03/12/14 05:34PM

Items Checked Out

Customer Number: 591294

The spoken word revolution redux /
33021021835969 Due: 04/02/14

Stage a poetry slam : creating performan
33021013363772 Due: 04/02/14

Total Checked Out: 2
****

Renew or reserve items online
at Anythinklibraries.org

*

*

calls anymore. He knows people will come because they heard "from Joanie, who heard from Bill that Bobby the harp player read a poem about Margaret, you remember Margaret, and she walked in and... Yeah! Out Loud! At Louie's! The Erotica Thing."

Don't confuse word of mouth with hype. Hype is what mega-entertainment moguls pour millions into to convince a gullible public that something unseen and untested is going to be the most sensational and rewarding experience of their lives. Sometimes it is, but usually it's not. Word of mouth is generated by people who have actually witnessed something sensational and feel an uncontrollable urge to pass it on—word of mouth doesn't cost a cent.

Almost anyone in the entertainment industry will testify that getting the buzz going outdistances any other form of advertisement by miles and dollars. How you get the buzz going is a combination of luck, persistence, and staging an impeccable show, week in and week out.

Press the Flesh

Hit the streets and start meeting fans, reporters, venue owners, and slammers face to face. A super way to promote your show in person is to attend special events. If a big poetry arts fair is coming town, make a point of attending it to pass out flyers, talk up your latest project, and show your support for what others in the community are doing.

Don't use another programmer's project selfishly to promote your own. Ask permission first. Most will say yes, but if they refuse, don't cop an attitude against them. It's their show and their right to say yes or no to anything that happens at it.

Louder Than a Bomb and the National Poetry Slam are events that poets and fans swarm to. What better place to meet people and introduce yourself and your new slam? Building an audience becomes a social activity with a marketing by-product, assuming you're graciously rigorous in your promotional quest; if you push your product enough and in the right way, they'll start coming to you.

Louder Than a Bomb is Chicago's annual teen slam competition sponsored by YCA (Young Chicago Authors, www.youngchicagoauthors.org). Each year dozens of high schools in and around Chicago send teams of poets to workshops, seminars, and competitions to celebrate spoken word.

Cool Calls

Some people break out in a cold sweat when they think of phoning people out of the icy blue. There's a reason for this—calling people out of the blue stinks. You catch people off guard or in the middle of work or dinner, if you catch them at all. With cell phones and caller ID, if the person you're calling doesn't recognize the number, he or she will usually choose to not pick up the phone. Who can blame them?

Phone solicitation is rapidly becoming a thing of the past, but the reason it's still done from time to time is simple: connect with an interested party and you're in. All the flyers in the world can be tossed in the garbage, but a human voice, given the chance, can nurture interest and cultivate it into commitment, in this case occupying a seat at your show. If you're seriously concerned that the word isn't getting out about a particular event, pick up the phone and start dialing. Ask your close buddies to do the same.

Don't call complete strangers, people who haven't the vaguest idea what a slam is. Reminding friends, fans, and potential fans that an event is around the corner sometimes puts folks on the spot, but it is often a welcomed nudge to the memory. Hard sell soliciting to strangers is just plain rude, and it might even get you into trouble with the law if the person is on a no-call list.

How Much Promoting...and to Whom?

Munich slammasters Rayl Patzak and Ko Bylanzky know that one of the mainstays of their monthly slams at the Substanz nightclub is the student body at Munich University. So during the school days preceding their Sunday show they spend hours placing hundreds of flyers on desktops in dozens of classrooms and standing in the hallways between classes passing out handbills. They know their target market, and they hit it hard. They also know that a percentage of their audience comes from the general population, so they seize every opportunity they can to score an article or interview in the daily or weekly newspapers, magazines, or radio shows.

The time and resources available for promoting your show are finite, so spend them wisely. Initiating a costly direct mail campaign to a thousand hunting enthusiasts (from the database you borrowed from your brother-in-law, the sports equipment salesman) might not be the smartest marketing approach for promoting your upcoming Save Bambi Poetry Hour.

The following sections offer some guidelines for arriving at a balanced equation between the time and resources you have at your disposal and how you effectively spend them.

How Many People Do You Need to Reach?

Your promotional needs vary according to the number of seats you need to fill. If your show is in a twenty-seat theater and you're staging a one-night test run of a work in progress, a few posters, word of mouth, and emailing your closest friends should be sufficient. But if your intention is to create an ongoing weekly slam, then press releases, a website (or blog), regular flyer distribution, and an Internet newsletter would be a minimum approach for securing enough audience to make your show a success.

Follow this simple rule of thumb: *expect only one of ten people you've reached through your promotional campaign to attend, and always do a little more advertising and promoting than you think necessary.*

If it seems like putting up fifty posters will cover the target areas of your campaign, put up seventy-five. If spending three hours a night (instead of two) calling friends will have a net gain of informing fifty more people about your debut slam, do it. Calculate the number of people you can fit into your venue, times that by the number of shows you're going to present, and then times that by the ten percent rule. This gives a good idea of how many flyers to print, people to call, and posters to hang to fill all the seats.

> Since the late '90s, virgin slams in midsize and smaller cities have been reporting initial audiences ranging from fifty to one hundred and fifty people. Expect an average of fifty heads and hearts to slip in through the doorway to check it out, but be prepared to cram in two hundred bodies if you have to.

Motivating Yourself with Deadlines

Deadlines are a necessary evil. You know them, you hate them, you avoid them, and you test their limits. Perhaps you simply need to look at them differently. Deadlines are your friends. They motivate you, keep you focused, and can actually free your procrastinating mind from having to recall the details of a task that needs to be done *now!*

Look at a calendar and set deadlines/goals for your project's marketing and promotional plans. Here are some examples of activities for which you might want to set deadlines:

- Design logo for new show
- Create flyers and postcards with branding logo on them
- Take flyer and postcard copy to printer
- Start composing press release
- Pick up flyers and postcards at printer
- Finalize press release
- Mail out postcards
- Start distributing flyers
- Mail out press releases
- Continue distributing flyers
- Make follow-up calls to press contacts

By setting deadlines (and meeting them), you're working within a defined time frame that nips at your heels. Without one it's too easy to procrastinate. For an independent project such as organizing a slam, you probably don't have to answer to anyone. No one's going to nag you to mail the postcards or punish you if the flyers aren't passed out. The consequence of not getting your promo out in a timely fashion is an empty house on opening night. To ensure that you have all the marketing materials you need when you need them and that all necessary promotional tasks are accomplished, jot down a checklist and assign a deadline to each and every item on your list. Use the deadlines to kick yourself in the pants when nobody else is around to do it for you.

The Push

Having slick marketing materials stacked on your kitchen table or boxed in the trunk of your car does nothing; you've got to GET THEM INTO THE HANDS OF THE PUBLIC! Email your announcements, hang your posters, leave small stacks of flyers in coffee shops and libraries, and talk, talk, talk up your show wherever you go. Even the grocery store clerk isn't safe from your advances. Be the Slam-Crier. Make sure everybody knows what's about to go down and give them good reason to get down with it. Let them know the time and place, and inspire them to pass it on to a friend who tells a friend, who...well, you get the idea.

Push hard toward the exciting homestretch—like a full-time/over-time/self-made marketing manic/obsessive by sending out press releases and postcards, plastering the bulletin boards with paper, scooting back and forth across the city scattering handbills in your wake, flyers and flyers, and more flyers, emailing, phone calling, and spilling your passions in interviews. Believe me, you'll be glad you did when all the seats are filled; you'll have no regrets about not doing enough.

> Ask for help. Recruit friends, fans, and slammers. Ask for an hour or two of their free time to help stuff envelopes or hang posters. Offer them free tickets to the show or free pizza and beer. Let them know that their help means a lot to you (it should) and that you want to compensate them for their efforts.

If you have a college or university nearby, consider taking on an intern. The English, performing arts, social services, and marketing departments all have creative students who are willing to work for a little on-the-job training and the prospect of establishing professional contacts.

And when the great push is over and you've had record-breaking ticket sales catapulting you and your slam into the realm of cult classics and filling the coffers with funds to fuel your next project:

- **Say Thank You.** It would be impossible to send thank-you notes to every person who came to see your show, but you can certainly thank the people who made the extra effort to help. You can also use your email list to send one general thank you. Make an extra effort to slobber thanks on your crew.

- **Update the mailing lists.** The sign-up list you set up in the lobby is no doubt full of new signatures. Add them to your database. They already did what you wanted them to do—and they'll do it again (assuming you put on a good show) and remind them of upcoming shows.

- **Follow up with the reporters.** Thank the reporters who wrote up your show before showtime and let them know of your show's success. They might just do a follow-up story (if they haven't already). Use the success of this show to generate interest in future shows.

- **Post about it on your blog.** If you have a blog, write a post describing the highlights (and perhaps low points) of the show. Remember, blogging is all about transparency, so if the performers stunk up the joint, don't pull your jabs. Hopefully, as in the case of many slams gone bad, the audience still had fun slamming the bad performances—write about that, too.

If you remember anything, remember...

- Before you start generating marketing materials, take time to define and describe your slam's essence and its main selling points.

- Choose marketing materials and media that will be most effective in reaching your target audience and inspiring their enthusiasm.

- Tap the power of the Internet by creating a website or blog, establishing a presence on social networking sites, and keeping in touch with patrons and poets via email.

- Great reviews and word-of-mouth advertising are your two most effective marketing tools—and they're free!

- Find a balanced equation between your marketing and promotional wish list and the time and financial resources available.

- Don't forget to follow up after the show, thanking those who helped, updating your mailing list, connecting with any reporters who helped spread the word, and posting highlights on your blog...if you have one.

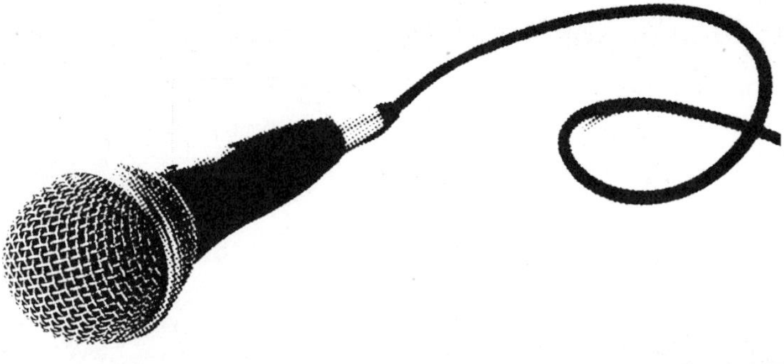

NEXT UP!

Courting the Institutions

Types of Institutions
Getting Your Iambic Toe in the Door
Book Fairs and Festivals
Corporate Conventions and Programming
Benefits and Their Paybacks

Shaping Your Show for the Expanded Market

Motorcycle Slam
Celebrity Slam
Slam Dunk Poetry Day

Other Twists

The Youth Slam
The Music + Poetry + Slam Slam
Bah! Humbug! The Holiday Slam

From Nothing Something Slams

Fat Tuesday Celebration of the Seven Deadly Sins

Chi Town Classic
Slammin' across America

Your Overall Strategy

If you remember anything, remember...

12 EXPANDING YOUR MARKET: SPECIAL SHOWS

Taverns, coffeehouses, nightclubs, and other small venues are the slam family's bread and butter. Over the years they have provided slammasters ideal arenas for creating poetic happenings, and have also become laboratories for experimenting with new show formats, rituals, and performers. In the process, they've exposed thousands of potential slam fans to the beauty and intensity of performance poetry.

Yet, these small venues represent only one slice of the slam pie—a big slice, but definitely not the whole cannoli. Other appealing and lucrative markets are out there waiting to be tapped. This chapter shows you where to look for them, how to approach their gatekeepers, and what to do to tailor your show to suit their special needs.

Courting the Institutions

Large institutions are always looking for new and exciting programming, especially in the literary arts department. Your slam can offer these institutions what they long for: entertaining, compelling, and accessible spoken word presentations that appeal to the general public. That's the key with large institutions—appealing to a broad spectrum of the population. Their target audience is everybody, and so is slam's.

After you've established a sound reputation and staged many successful shows, arrange your marketing evidence into a compelling bouquet and start knocking on the big doors of culture. The major cultural institutions and associations have the cash to underwrite ambitious projects—budgets fattened by big donors, access to government funding, and foundations set up to keep them churning out programming for the masses. Fees for creating and producing poetry events to fit their needs and desires can range from a few hundred to thousands of dollars.

Approach "literary" institutions with caution, humility, grace, and a thick skin. Many have a built-in bias against anything slam. They are either jealous of what the "unlettered" slam community has accomplished or misinformed about what slam really is. Sometimes they've had a bad experience at a pseudo slam or with a slam personality operating in contradiction to the tenets presented in this book. Have your marketing materials in tow when you call on them with plenty of testimonies from the organizations you've worked for and pleased.

Types of Institutions

Don't limit your courtships. Slammin' at the Northwest Cattle Breeders Association? Why not? I've been hired by Commonwealth Edison, Kraft Foods, and several other large corporations to create poetry shows during the lunch hours to give their employees a much needed creative boost and shake off their workday doldrums. What better way to charge things up than with a poetry slam?

How do you find these gigs? Where do you look? Here are some obvious choices. Use them as a starting point, not an end:

- Associations, such as the National Association of Speech Therapists or the National Association of Librarians... Psychologists...Bookbinders, you name it, all hold annual conventions and are always seeking out fun and thoughtful activities for their members to enjoy.

- Cultural arts centers can be found in almost every midsized city and in all major metropolitan areas. Their purpose is to find and create a wide variety of arts programming, and they are usually struggling to fill their calendars with the required number of literary arts events.

- Museums, big and small, have programming throughout the year connected to different themes and exhibits. If you can shape a slam event to fit one of their themes, you're in. Museums typically pay well and provide high-profile exposure through their elaborate advertising campaigns. An added benefit is that your show will probably play to a new audience of potential slam converts. If you do a good job, you'll get asked back for their next special event and possibly draw a few converts to your venue.

- Libraries usually have events once or twice a year that are linked to some national, state, or locally designated day or month, such as Dogpatch Days or National Fried Steak Week. April is National Poetry month and it's a big time for library events and the performance poets that work them. They have smaller budgets than museums, but bigger libraries can sometimes put on big shows. After you've done a good job, it almost always leads to repeat engagements.

Getting Your Iambic Toe in the Door

The downside of seeking institutional work is that it's a who-knows-whom situation. If your name and your slam logo have been splashed across the front page of the Arts section of the *Metropolitan News* for eight weeks running, then maybe you've got a shoe in the door. But if you're a humble show maker operating under the big scene radar, securing a gig on a cold call is iffy. Sending a press pack and a query letter is little more than a shot in the dark. But do it anyway; it's the first step. And if you are met with no response, try some of these tactics:

- Track down the director of your city's cultural arts center and send her a letter of introduction.

- Volunteer your services to the institution you're courting. Give them a taste of who you are and what you can do. Get to know who does what and how it gets done.

- Invite program directors to attend your monthly slam and give them the red carpet treatment. Heck, invite the whole department and give them front rows seats and personalized poems performed on their tabletop.

- Offer your services to programming boards. As a slammaster, you come in contact with lots of talent, and you're connected to a big family of performers across the country and around the world. You're a valuable resource to the programming folks.

Once you're on the inside, be ready to fit your show vision (for a fair price) into one of the institution's programming slots. If it turns out to be a smashing success, more opportunities will surely come your way.

In the spring of 1990, I offered to manage a citywide slam tournament to support Chicago's new Sister Cities program, the "Poem for Osaka Award." This donation of time and effort was rewarded later that year when Lois Weisberg, Commissioner of Chicago Cultural Affairs suggested (and paid for) a team of Chicago slammers to fly to San Francisco and compete in the first national slam competition. Over the years, I've been contracted to do more than a hundred events at Chicago's Cultural Center and have donated back an equal amount of time. Give to your local arts associations and you—as well as your community—shall truly receive.

Book Fairs and Festivals

As the slam has grown and gained more international visibility, book fairs and literary festivals have sought it out to add some spark to their events. Because slammers and slammasters know how to organize, they bring a readymade arts and entertainment package, easy-to-plug into the festival itinerary and guaranteed to pull in a new young audience.

If you do a book fair or festival gig, be sure to have a lot of flyers on hand to promote any projects you've got brewing. Participating in these events can be a great opportunity to expose a large audience to slam and to your regular weekly or monthly shows. Get that mailing list out and gather names and addresses. Sell T-shirts and CDs. These fairs and festivals are open marketplaces. Make the best of them.

Corporate Conventions and Programming

Similar to associations, major corporations hold conventions and need fun activities for their conventioneers to participate in when the day's meetings are over. Sometimes they're enlightened enough to seek out something other than a stand-up comedian spewing dirty jokes and golf anecdotes. Slam provides an entertaining, intellectually stimulating alternative.

Developing a relationship with a major corporation can lead to the sponsorship of events unrelated to their in-house corporate functions. Many forward thinking companies have philanthropic departments with the sole purpose of helping the arts and giving back to the communities that bolster their success by buying their products and services.

> Specialty acts such as jugglers and magicians work the corporate circuit extensively. If you have a friend in that line of work, ask your pal for the inside scoop.

Benefits and Their Paybacks

The old adage "it's better to give than to receive" sometimes transforms into "give a lot, get a lot." By volunteering your services and performing at benefits or for social institutions, you gain exposure that leads to more contacts and opportunities that can help your own projects. Many times small activist organizations grow into major ones, and they often remember and reward your early assistance. It's very easy to get involved—show up at the door and offer your services. Believe me, you won't be turned away.

> Be careful when donating your time, talents, and energy to just any organization. Some benefits and charity events are bogus, poorly run, and outlandish fronts for lining some unscrupulous organizer's pockets. Check the organization's credentials before lending your aid.

Shaping Your Show for the Expanded Market

You just got off the phone with the president of the local chapter of the Harley Hogs. You've been negotiating with them for weeks about helping them stage A Free Rider Festival of Motorcyclist Poetry, and they've finally said okay, the gig is yours. Now what? Should you rework your Save the Whales Slam to fit in with the biker theme or go back to the drawing board for a fresh start? You've got only three weeks to put it all together, and if you don't deliver on your promises... well...they're bikers.

Don't freak out. This is an opportunity to be creative and dig up artistic treasures you never knew were buried deep below the surface of your soul. Start with the basic slam as a foundation and build from there using the theme of the particular event as your guide. The following sections give you an idea how the basic slam structure can be reshaped to create exciting programming for special institutions.

Motorcycle Slam

Yes, I did create and stage a motorcycle slam, but not for bikers. In January of 1999, the Chicago's Field Museum of Natural History commissioned me to produce a special program to augment the Guggenheim Museum's traveling exhibit "Art of the Motorcycle."

A portable stage was erected on the main floor of the museum. A band of experimental musicians filled the hall with rhythms emanating from drums, guitars, and homemade instruments that resembled bicycle wheels. The plan was to open with the music and conduct a slam competition on the theme of speed, power, and freedom alternating between experienced slammers and audience members who were asked to compose fill-in-the-blank poems handed out to them as they sat down to listen to the wild music emanating from the experimental band.

Don't start thinking the Chicago slammers are wussies donning costumes to *play* at being hard case bikers. In the early 1990s, accepting an invitation they couldn't refuse, Jean Howard and Rob Van Tuyle, members of the Chicago Poetry Ensemble, staged several slam events for the Chicago Outlaws Motorcycle Club at their concrete bunker headquarters. Rival clubs gathered to watch men with names like Apehanger and No Tooth read poetry about riding free. The men couldn't top the scores that the bikini clad women got for reading rhymes about...well...just use your imagination.

Streams of Midwesterners climbed up and down the huge marble staircases at each end of the Grand Hall. Nuns, boy scouts, Indiana State young republicans, truck-driving daddies with strings of kids, and truck-driving mamas with teenaged daughters—they were all there. Between each tune (to build suspense) I apologized to the audience for the late start.

"Sorry folks, the biker poets aren't here yet. You know how bikers are—very independent, big, and scary. We're hoping that they'll show up, but..."

After the third apology, an air horn blasted on the Grand Staircase and into the Grand Hall. Under the bones of a dinosaur's neck, a crew of slammers clad in black leather, chains, and Harley Davidson emblems clanked their way through the open-mouthed crowd. After another blast from the air horn, they started blaring poetry over their hand-held bullhorns.

That was the beginning of the "Spoke 'N Word Poetry Slam." The afternoon included ensemble performances by slam pros, the impromptu fill-in-the-blank open-mic competition by audience members, and the music. A twelve-year-old soon-to-be-biker won the prize. His power poem is long lost in the exhaust fumes, but you can try creating one yourself.

The Power Poem
To each and every life there comes
An hour when timidity no longer rules.
And when that time arrives at last
Give me power to ______________________ (verb)
And power to ________________________ (verb)
Power that ______________ (adv.)
_______________ (verb)
Every _________ (noun) that ever __________ (verb)
Oh yes, Power is the goddess!
Power is the king!
Give me that _______________ (lots of adjectives)
Powerful thing!

Celebrity Slam

For several years I helped create and produce a benefit for The Three Arts Club of Chicago, an institution that supported female artists and performers. The centerpiece of these nights of food and entertainment were celebrity slams. We recruited radio personalities to create poems for the SOUND BITE SLAM. Here's how it worked: Each of six radio personalities composed a 30-second, 60-second, and 120-second poem about the benefit's theme and performed their poems in a three-round slam bout. Judges were chosen from the audience and were very excited to be in such close proximity to their local radio heroes.

You might think that convincing a world-renowned entertainer or a local celebrity to perform at your show would be a monumental task, but many big-name performers need you just as much as you need them. Don't assume that your city's mayor, the local football coach, Cher, or Bill Gates wouldn't be interested in slammin' for the fun of it and to help a cause. Call them. You'd be surprised at how many closet poets are out there. After their names are on the roster, you can bet on a standing-room-only house. I haven't heard of Madonna getting in on the slam *yet,* but she obviously doesn't know what she's missing.

Former Philadelphia Eagles running back Cecil Martin organized and participated in (as a poet, not a running back) a slam benefit for the Evanston, Illinois YWCA. Ray Suarez of National Public Radio fame hosted a kids vs. pros (U.S. Poet Laureate Robert Hass, Nikki Giovanni, and a few others) slam in Washington D.C. to benefit The Writers Corporation. Viggo Mortensen, film star of *Lord of the Rings,* unveiled his art and poetry at a slam-related event to benefit San Francisco-based Youth Speaks. All these big names donated their time for poetry and a good cause.

Slam Dunk Poetry Day

An ensemble of local and national slam poets assembled in Chicago for a day-long event to celebrate a traveling poetry and photo exhibit based upon John Huet's and Jimmy Smith's book *Soul of the Game.*

The day culminated in a slam competition between two teams of slam greats performing solos, duets, and trios. A team would "shoot" by performing a poem. The opposing team could then try to "block the shot" by performing a short improvisational verse based on the same theme and gaining the crowd's approval by applause. Judges held up cards that read "Slam Dunk" 3 points, "Score" 2 points, or "Stuff" 1 point, and, of course, if your poem was blocked by audience applause, 0 points.

Other Twists

Your slam is a hit—or at least everyone involved, including the audience, thinks it's grand, but something seems to be missing. It just doesn't snap and sizzle for you anymore. You and it are in a rut. Both you and your show need a good old fashioned cold shower, a jump in the sea,—something to wash the cobwebs from your brain and draw some fresh faces to the crowd. This is a good sign that you need to juice up your weekly slam with a special event or a different set of rules. Think of this one-shot show as a holiday special or a two-hour episode of your favorite TV show. Everyone will tune in because they want to see something new and different infused with the energy of your innovative mind. The following sections offer some inspiration.

The Youth Slam

Youth slams are hot. The next generation of poets are already starting slams coast to coast and creating communities of unique, fresh voices. Slam is taught in workshops in high school and junior high school, in libraries, and in after-school programs as an effective means to get kids talking, creating, and sharing their thoughts and feelings. Every year the National Youth Slam is held in a different city in America. When they say "youth," they mean it—unless you're between thirteen and nineteen years old, you're not qualified. The venues are in coffeehouses and other nondrinking, nonsmoking venues, of course, and the slams are just as exciting as any other slams. You'll keep asking yourself, "Why wasn't I doing this when I was their age?" Borrow on the youth idea to create a special-ages show at your event.

The national youth slam, traveling under the name of Brave New Voices, was the brainchild of Connecticut slammer Elizabeth Thomas. Over its ten-year history it has grown to include several youth organizations that coproduce the event. For more information, visit www.upwordspoetry.com and click the link for Brave New Voices.

The Music + Poetry + Slam Slam

What do you get when you make a poet use music in his piece? Occasionally, you get a train wreck. Many times, though, you get a lovely marriage of spoken word and music that no one (including you) ever expected. Holding an "All Poets Must Groove with the Band" Slam might not be an option for some venues—many slams these days use a DJ to supply tunes or simply throw a few CDs in the blender and hit "play." However, some venues have live musicians in house, and if you have the chance to host a slam with a band or the opportunity to perform with one, do it.

Do you have a sad, melancholy poem? Ask the band to play "My Funny Valentine." Got an angry, "give-me-my-stuff-back" poem? Sex Pistols. You'll be surprised at what transpires. The best part about a Band Slam is that it adds a new element of competition—maybe your poem is great, and maybe your performance is good, but can you play well with others?

In France, the word "slam" has become as familiar to the general public as the term "hip hop" thanks to recording artist Grand Corps Malade (www.grandcorpsmalade.com), a young man who started combining his poetry with music at a local slam in Paris and has now become a spoken word superstar.

Bah! Humbug! The Holiday Slam

Just when you couldn't stand any more holiday cheer, you see that your favorite poetry venue is holding a Holiday Slam. What can you do? Go home and dust off that punk version of *A Christmas Carol* you scratched onto a piece of dark metal one bitter winter night or compose a verse explaining what the Easter Bunny should do with those eggs. A lot of slam venues hold special Holiday Slams. Often the cover charge for such events is a nonperishable food item or a pair of mittens. Any money collected is donated to a good cause. During the holidays, many slammasters have lent their skills and slams to help the less fortunate.

From Nothing Something Slams

Perceiving and filling a need is a basic business concept that applies to creating new slam shows, as well. A particular section of the community yearns for a slam that focuses more on *their* sensibilities and that doesn't fit the current slam atmosphere existing in their town. Maybe they want a "We Read Off the Paper—Non-Memorized Slam" or the "Politics Are Not Our Game Slam." The need could be related to an untapped resource; for instance, a large community of short story writers with no place to speak their works—"The North Shore Story Slam."

Recognizing a potential need takes a keen eye—an ability to step back and see what others are missing. Of course, I can't give you specifics on what your community needs, but take a look at the real-life examples described in the following sections.

Fat Tuesday Celebration of the Seven Deadly Sins

For some time I had been running a slam in the suburbs of Chicago in conjunction with the Sunday show at the Green Mill. I wanted to create a special show to boost weekly attendance at the Tuesday night West Side Poetry Slam. I reasoned that people love to celebrate special occasions, so I started to think about calendar dates and holidays. A Christmas slam? No, everyone has a special Christmas show, and the same was true for Halloween. Good Friday/Easter weekend was another obvious choice. How 'bout the Dog Days of August Slam? Wait a minute! Mardi Gras! Fat Tuesday! That's it!

When I created the Fat Tuesday Celebration of the Seven Deadly Sins, there were absolutely no high-profile Fat Tuesday celebrations in Chicago. It was a big gaping hole, an unperceived need that has since been filled up with numerous Fat Tuesday events after the Sin Slam paved the way.

The event proved to be a spectacular sold-out performance of seven poetry ensembles, each creating a 12-minute "poetry parade" based on one of the seven deadly sins. They were encouraged to use costumes, props, and music. One memory that stands out is the Sloth "krewe" being wheeled in on hospital gurneys performing their poems from the prone position because they were too lazy to get out of bed.

A *krewe* is a social organization that stages a parade or a ball as part of a Mardi Gras celebration. Krewe members typically ride on the floats during a parade. For our Fat Tuesday Celebration of the Seven Deadly Sins, we treated each team of performers as a krewe.

The Fat Tuesday celebration was so successful I was encouraged by poets and audience to restage it annually. It ran for six years and produced songs, poems, and stunts unmatched in slam history for their audacity and daring. All of it grew out of a need to boost attendance at the weekly show and fill an empty spot in the holiday schedule.

Chi Town Classic

Krystal Ashe, who for years produced one of Chicago's spin-off slams, recognized the potential of creating a grand slam event on the Thursday preceding the annual slammasters meeting in Chicago. She reasoned quite correctly that all this great talent from across the country would be in town for the meetings, so why not schedule a performance to benefit PSI? At the Chi Town Classic, Chicago slammers pair off against slammers and slammasters from around the country for a king-of-the-hill slam extravaganza.

Be on the lookout for book fairs, author conventions, and literary conferences, such as those sponsored by the AWP (Association of Writers & Writing Programs, www.awpwriter.org). These literary celebrations and get-togethers could be prime occasions for creating fringe events like the Chi Town Classic to make the most of the out-of-town talent gathering in your own backyard. Your town may also have its own unique literary fairs, such as Chicago's Printers Row Book Fair.

> Newspapers love to cover special events. They might be reluctant to cover your weekly slam, even if it's the best matching of local poets ever. But make it a special occasion and give it an event angle—"Poet Titans meet Poet Godzillas for the First Time"—and the press will do it up right.

Slammin' across America

Gary Glazner, the passion and promotion behind the First National Slam, provided the business savvy to create and ramrod the 2000 Slam America Tour. Over one hundred poets participated in this

Ken Kesey–style bus tour (minus most of the drugs), which covered over eight thousand miles, thirty-two cities, and thirty-six readings in thirty days. Grand Marnier sponsored the tour through PSI along with support from Manic D Press, publisher of Gary's book, *Poetry Slam, The Competitive Art of Performance Poetry.* Slam America Tour showcased the performance aspect of Slam Poetry and inspired the following show formats used to excite crowds along its route:

- The Haiku Death Match evolved from Gary's hosting of Haiku Slams at the Nationals. It is a fast-paced exchange of haiku punctuated with audience chants of HI-KU, HI-KU, HI-KU. At the end, one of the poets would feign committing hari-kari.

- The Yo Mama Samurai Skits are based on the old Japanese Samurai movies where the voices were out of sync. Two poets offstage using microphones provide the dialog, and two poets onstage act out the scene and try to keep up with the words. If it is done well, the audience has a hard time telling who is speaking.

The Slam America Tour was a huge success. It played down the competition and played up the theatrics of performance, dispelling the image of poetry as a dry and dusty art.

Television, radio, and print media coverage of the tour reached over five million people; and bus driver, Paul Cavendish, started speaking haiku about halfway through the tour.

Your Overall Strategy

Whether you're pitching your slam to the board members of your local public library system, the CEO of a large corporation, or the programming director of the cultural arts center, your strategy is the same: provoke their imagination and then implant your vision in their brains. You want the vision of your slam playing like a movie on the inner wall of their skulls. Then, after you've hooked them, make them believe that you can pull it off.

Programming people want to be inspired, convinced, and then, once sold, they want to leave it all to you. Take charge. Don't expect the institution director or her assistants to tell you what to do or how to do it. They're providing you with time and space in their schedule, and back-up support. And sometimes that support doesn't include all the cash needed, so part of your job might be finding supplemental financing or a least a scheme of how to make ends meet. Get to work. Attend to every last detail or delegate tasks to people you trust, making sure that whomever you've delegated a duty to does it. A hassle-free night of fine art entertainment will keep you in the slam producing business for a long time.

If you remember anything, remember...

- Although the small venues are your meat and potatoes, special shows, benefits, and appearances at institutions can add gravy, spices, and delicious desserts to your visions.

- Look to museums, libraries, associations, and your town's cultural arts center for opportunities to stage your show.

- Corporations are always looking for entertaining, imaginative, illuminating presentations to refresh and inspire their employees.

- For most institutional presentations, you must tailor your show to appeal specifically to the institution's audience or to a particular event or situation.

- You can breathe new life into your weekly show by staging a holiday show or one-time special that changes your slam's focus or follows a different set of rules.

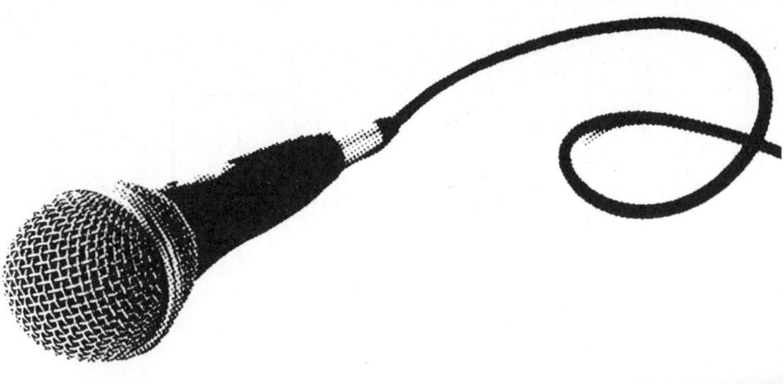

NEXT UP!

When All Is Said and Done... Do More

Greeting Your Guests with Grace and Grin

Introducing Guest to Guest

Acting as the Maître D'

Setting a Stage, Not a Pedestal

Watch the Clock—Starting on Time

Fueling Audience Frenzy

Making the Most of a $lam $ituation

Preserving the History

Creating Anthologies

Burning Compilation CDs

Designing T-Shirts and Souvenirs

Establishing Profitable Partnerships

Absurd Ambitions and Other Worldly Temptations

If you remember anything, remember...

13 TAKING OWNERSHIP OF YOUR SHOW

You're the consummate puppet master. You invented and organized a first-class show and promoted the heck out of it. You delegated the duties of door person, ticket taker, emcee, sign-up secretary, scorekeeper, audio technician, and lighting expert to trusted members of your crew. You're a behind-the-scenes type and you like it that way. Now you're ready to kick back with your favorite beverage and watch the majesty of the evening unfold before you.

Not so fast! Your pilot and crew may run the show brilliantly, but you still need to stand at the helm.

Responsible and professional helpers appreciate a visible captain and usually need (or want) to demonstrate their expertise to the person in charge. You're the foundation upon which they stand. When you're there they feel secure, when you're not they feel abandoned. In addition, you have a responsibility to make your guests feel at home, and that's essential for making any slam succeed. This chapter shows you how to continue to play an active role as slammaster even when all is smooth-sailing on automatic pilot.

When All Is Said and Done...Do More

Slam night again. The venue manager has carefully arranged the tables and chairs for maximum eye contact with the performers. He has pulled out the risers and assembled the portable stage. Your lighting technician, doubling as sound geek, climbs the ladder, focuses the lights, and balances the EQ. You set up the ticket table and stock it with programs, chapbooks, and T-shirts to sell. Everything's in place.

All this hard work was overwhelming weeks ago, but now it's routine. You could just sit on a stool and blink things into place while melting into the wallpaper, but don't. Your job as slammaster is to make your guests feel toasty, encourage their participation, and find new ways to celebrate performance poetry and serve its audience. The following sections show you how to go about establishing a good rapport with the audience and fostering the sense of community that really makes a show take off.

Greeting Your Guests with Grace and Grin

As the patrons begin to enter, stand by the door and say "Howdy. Welcome. What up?" A few first-timers will look at you like you're some kind of goof but so what? By the end of the slam they'll understand that it's all part of the game. And if they don't? Que sera, you'll never see them again.

After you "howdy" the arrivals, ask them if they're poets and have a poem to perform. "Yes!" Sign 'em up. "No, just here to listen? Well, you're the most important element of the night." It's true. Without an audience poets are just howling in a dark, lonely, who-cares room. Slams are active, powered by the energy of the performer/audience interaction. By greeting folks you're sparking the fuse that's about to blast your show wide open.

Introducing Guest to Guest

When you're not at the door greeting people, work the crowd. Introduce one table of veterans to a neighboring table of virgins and have them all shout "Yo!" across the room to the visitors from France. By introducing people, you're forming a community, breaking down inhibitions, loosening tongues, and priming your audience to respond and react to what they're about to witness. The more the audience reacts, the more rewarding the show will be for all.

Try this experiment once, *just once.* Start your show without introducing folks to one another. Observe how the first set goes, how responsive the audience is. At the first break, go around and actively greet and introduce people as described above—focus on the people you thought were particularly reserved. Start the second set and see how things change. I'll bet the second set is fueled with more fervor than the first.

Acting as the Maître D'

At the Green Mill it's almost always standing room only, so the manager and I seat people to make sure all the booths, stools, and tables are used to their capacity. This has turned into a great opportunity for us to help audience members connect to one another. Someone passes a chair or scoots over to make room for a solo newcomer, their eyes meet, they exchange a few words, and all of a sudden they're connected.

Eighty percent of the time, a chance encounter transforms acquaintances into comrades, like a wedding table of strangers who have a grand time during the reception in contrast to the grumbling in-laws and bickering siblings. If you have the opportunity to act as maître d' at your show, make the most of it.

Setting a Stage, Not a Pedestal

The stage might raise you, your emcee, and your performers above the level of the audience, but don't let it go to your head or the heads of your performers. The stage is raised only so the audience can see. If the onstage personalities start to think they're better than the offstage people who come to see them, all sorts of problems rear up and bray.

As slammaster, you're going to earn a degree in psychology from the college of hard knocks and knuckleheads. You're going to meet (and have to deal with) a host of personalities from pleasant to repulsive, from gracious to hideous, from responsible to reckless. As time goes on, you'll weed out the arrogant and unreliable performers and cultivate a garden of fine performers you can rely on to be punctual, courteous, and incredibly engaging onstage. Until then, be prepared to encounter a few of these less attractive personality types:

- **The Apologizer:** Late, unprepared, and generally incompetent, the apologizer is always sorry and says so as easily as saying "Hello." "Sorry I'm late." "Sorry my piece bombed so bad—next time I'll rehearse." Tell the apologizer what you think, what you expect, and that if it happens again, they might want to consider performing solo on a street corner in another town.

- **The Blamer:** When something goes wrong, the blamer is never at fault. "Man, you need to work on your sound system." "If you would've given me that third slot, I'd have kicked rump." "Your whole vision for this show is screwed up." Assuming the criticism is unfounded, encourage the blamer to perform at some better shows. However, if the blamer is right, ask for advice—you might be able to improve your show.

- **God's Gift to Slam:** The arrogant slammer is one of the most obnoxious personalities you'll meet. This slammer thinks that you, your crew, the audience, and the club owner should bow down and pay homage to the master. Maybe God's Gift to Slam really is a great poet and performer, but the truly greats are typically humble, and they treat others with respect. If you encounter a God's Gift to Slam who's good, a little advice on honing people skills might be useful. If they're mediocre (or downright awful) and continue to treat you, your audience, or your crew disrespectfully, show God's Gift the door.

- **The Interrogator:** The Interrogator has no self-confidence and peppers you with questions throughout the evening just to get some attention. "When do I go on? Who's going on before me? Where can I set up my stuff? Can my friends get in free? Can you adjust the lights just so? Where's the dressing room?" Of course, many of these questions are valid, but they should have been addressed before (not during) the show. If you have several Interrogators, it might be a good sign that you need to type up an information sheet for performers. If the Interrogator keeps asking the same questions and follows you around like a lost puppy, shake him, fast.

- **Slam Cop:** A stickler for the rules, the Slam Cop is going to point out every digression from the official rules, no matter how miniscule the infraction. At national competitions, this might be welcomed, to a point, but if you're trying to foster an informal atmosphere at a local club, the Slam Cop can become an annoying control freak. Explain what you're trying to do and why you're allowing rules to be bent and broken. If that doesn't make him back off, take a more direct approach—suggest that he start his own show.

Watch the Clock—Starting on Time

One of the traits of poorly structured poetry events is that they rarely start on time and usually run way past their welcome. People start looking at their watches and wiggling in their seats, the reading becomes drawn out and watered down, and the whole experience loses its intensity. Develop a reputation for starting on time and ending before the audience is exhausted. Let everyone know up front that "tonight's show will include Mop Head Jake and the Steel Drum Dubs followed by the Diva Demon Slam Finals" and that everything's going to whirl along across the next two hours and conclude no later than 11:00.

A ten-minute hold for latecomers or to allow a few more seats to fill is okay, now and then, and even traditional in some theater circles. But once a late start becomes habitual, patrons and performers start showing up later and later. All that becomes a drag on the show's potential.

Nothing is more discouraging to an audience than a show that starts late. Think about attending a play and waiting an hour for the curtain to rise—it would be unbearable. It's a little more tolerable in a bar where you can buy a drink and play some jukebox tunes. But a large percentage of first-time audience members won't tolerate late starts, and the negative word of mouth they generate will eventually chip away at your show's reputation.

Fueling Audience Frenzy

Sometimes a show just can't find the high gear. Either the open micers were all somber or the special guest went flat as a pep-less Dr. Pepper—no fizzle, no sizzle, no spark. A big bland blah. You could just chalk it up to experience and look to jazz up next week's show. But why let the entire evening flop? Dig down in that show-master toolbox of yours, pull out your jumper cables, and zap the seats with jump juice. Here are a few suggestions for pumping life into a dying show:

- Have one of your more accomplished open mic regulars stand up unannounced in the audience and belt out a short exclamatory poem, "Oh Thou Mighty Muse within My

Mighty Pen!" Usually a loud, high-energy piece is the best for this, but tenderness has worked. Ask the poet to keep it under two minutes—you're looking for intensity here, short and punchy, not ponderously profound.

- Recruit several open micers or your in-house ensemble to knock out a round robin (as described in Chapter 6), emoting from around the room and on the stage. Planned or impromptu, a round robin is an easy and exciting way to stoke the flames of audience interest.

- Stage an across-the-room duet. Have two of your better performers with strong voices position themselves at opposite ends of the room and present line by line or stanza by stanza a lacework of two poems that have thematic or stylist connections. Be sure there's some lighting focused on them and that they're clearly visible. To make this stunt effective, the performers must speak and respond directly to each other, creating an intimate scene that the audience is privy to—like eavesdropping on poets in the heavens playing out their passions and words.

The first across-the-room duet I encountered was performed by two eighth graders in a workshop I conducted. They stood atop the tables in the school library and delivered a poem about the struggles of their friendship. All of us were hushed and almost in tears at its end. I've used the technique in shows ever since.

- Initiate a *call and response*. You can do this with your in-house ensemble or with the audience. Have in your repertoire a poem that calls for the audience to respond with words or whistles or groans. You've seen this done a million times at church, at concerts, and at political rallies. Invent your own call and response tricks and keep them handy.

- Be a momentary BIG MOUTH. Sometimes all an audience needs to smash their inhibitions is to hear someone else get vocal. A word or three in response to a poet's offering onstage can open the door. If you think you might be too conspicuous doing it yourself, find an eager friend to serve as the ringer. It's a blast.

A little BIG MOUTH goes a long way. Don't disrupt a performance, however weak, with loud, smarmy interjections. Use your big mouth to spark some energy in the gaps between poems and then...hush.

- If you've got a real brave soul in your ensemble, send him up to the stage to be purposely awful, to invoke the snap, the groan, and/or the feminist hiss, laying the groundwork for authentic audience retaliation against the drones of a failing open mic.

Making the Most of a $lam $ituation

Genuine poets and slammasters don't like to treat their artistic creations like run of the mill "products" to be hawked like trinkets outside a ballpark or county fair. Their art is as important to them as their souls. That doesn't mean they don't like to make money. As long as they remain true to their vision, many slammasters and slammers serve the patrons by offering quality chapbooks, anthologies, CDs, T-shirts, and other merchandise. The following sections provide some ideas to help you develop your own product line.

Preserving the History

Establish a system for preserving the history of your show. If you've already staged a few shows, it's not too late to start. Keep a journal, audio recordings, and, if possible, video-tapings or digital records of your shows. These audio and video recordings can also provide the raw materials you need to create anthologies—collections of your slam's best performances.

> Don't subject your audience to a tactless, shaky video cameraman who gets in their way or distracts them with noisy, clumsy movements. If you videotape your shows make sure the equipment and operators are as inconspicuous and considerate as possible. And please no glaring lights!

Of course, when you're playing the role of slammaster, you can't possibly videotape the show yourself. Find someone who loves your slam and is bubbling with the passion to record it. They're out there. Turn over the reins to them. Having a camcorder running inspires and rewards your performers and adds an aura of importance to your show. (See Chapter 10 wherein I encourage you to recruit a volunteer to function as your show's slam historian.)

Creating Anthologies

Desktop publishing is commonplace now. With relative ease a slammaster or someone in her crew can collect poems from the slammers and assemble them into a chapbook anthology. Here are the steps:

1. Collect the poems you want to include and obtain permission from the poets to use them in your anthology. (Get permissions in writing.)

2. Work with the poets to edit the selections into an acceptable page form.

> Get ready for some sloppy manuscripts (or no manuscripts at all) from some of your favorite performers. Many performers, myself included, do not actively seek publication, and their poems evolve onstage to forms that have no page equivalent. As editor you'll be guiding some slammers through the page process.

3. Assemble the selections into some kind of logical order—alphabetically by poet or subject matter, by date of performance, or according to some other system.

4. Lay out the poems in a book format (or have someone else do it). Use a computer equipped with a good desktop publishing program.

5. Find an artist to design a book cover.

6. Compile and create the incidentals: table of contents, acknowledgements, title page, graphics, forward, and so on. Check out a couple poetry anthologies and see what incidentals they include.

7. Get some price quotes from local printers and find out how they want the originals delivered. Can you submit the book electronically—on CD or via the Internet? Do you need to submit it in print, as *page proofs?* What size? If you're doing color, how must you do the color separations? If you don't know anything about printing, don't try to fake it; admit your total ignorance and let the printer explain things to you.

Page proofs are the final final printouts of a publication that are ready to be reproduced at the printers to create bound versions.

8. Put your baby into production and plan a release party, and don't forget to issue a press release announcing its birth. (For more about press releases and other marketing tools, check out Chapter 11, "Getting the Word Out: Publicizing Your Show.")

Unless your anthology is being released through a major publishing house, there is little or no payment you can offer the contributors. (You'll be lucky to break even.) It's a labor of love; most poets realize this and are happy just to have their poems honored in print. If someone demands payment that you cannot guarantee, omit their works. Giving your contributors a set number of free copies, however, is expected, and if you should sell out the first edition and make a cool thousand fish or so, have a party for your poets to pay them back.

Editor Mark Eleveld's best-selling anthologies *The Spoken Word Revolution* and *The Spoken Word Revolution Redux* are being used in schools and universities throughout the world as guides to slam and performance poetry. They include CD compilations from performances recorded at slams around the world.

Burning Compilation CDs

Almost every touring poet has two or more CDs featuring their performances. It's just about as easy to make a CD compilation as it is to make a print anthology, probably easier, especially if you forgo including a text of the poems in the *liner notes*. Reproduction companies like Disc Makers (www.discmakers.com) will send you catalogues that give you the step by step, and sometimes a sales rep will guide you through them.

If they don't, the following steps describe the overall process:

1. Select the recorded performances you want to include. They may come from the nightly recordings you've done of your show, from CDs already produced by others, or from recordings made by the poets themselves, or you may record poets in your or a friend's studio.

2. Arrange the recordings into some logical order.

3. Find an artist to design the cover art and lay out the liner notes following the file formats provided by the reproduction company. Get them working on it.

4. Enlist the service of or employ a professional sound engineer to mix the tracks and lay them down on a mastered disc. The sound engineer must provide certain technical information about the recordings to the reproduction company to get the job done properly, so it's best to hire a professional.

5. Deliver the master disc, layout, and artwork to the production company. Send them a check and wait 2 to 6 weeks for your first CD compilation disc.

Anticipate having to make a host of production choices concerning liner notes, types of jewel cases, and artwork. You can ask and answer questions about such matters over the phone or through email with a sales rep for the reproduction company. They're in business to do everything for you. Pick their brains.

Designing T-Shirts and Souvenirs

Many local slams and every national slam event produce T-shirts to promote and commemorate their events. And because the slam is still hovering above the grass roots level and well below super mainstream radar, almost all of these T-shirts become collector's items. But slammers and slammasters have not stopped there—they've used their creative juices to stir up some kitschy new options you might consider for promoting your slam and just being goofy:

- **Cartoon strips and comic books.** It's been done, but it's never been taken as far as it could go. Imagine Poetic Action Heroes and the drama of their performance unfolding in each frame.

- **Trading cards.** Charles Ellik and the California poets started this. There's no reason why each local slam couldn't have its own deck of poet trading cards.

- **More stuff.** Bumper stickers. Tattoos. Pennants. Baseball caps. Bowling shirts. Poetic slippers.

Go for it. And make it fun. All these products help promote your show and create physical emblems of belonging for the slam community you're building.

Establishing Profitable Partnerships

Once your slam is cruising along and you've established an audience, it's time to hook up with other literary arts organizations in your city. They may have been critical of your early efforts, but set that aside, and work with them to:

- Bring in special guest performers

- Stage special citywide festivals

- Create workshops and outreach programs

- Share advertising expenses

Most literary arts establishments and cultural institutions are heavily supported by grants and governmental funding. They have the financial resources, and you have, if you've followed the slam path, a strong audience base. Hook up with them and see what can happen. The point is not you versus them, the point is poetry.

Absurd Ambitions and Other Worldly Temptations

The slam has not gone mainstream, but some of its family members have capitalized on great opportunities offered to them by mainstream commercial entities. Performance poets who got a big boost from local and national slams have obtained recording contracts, TV sitcom roles, book contracts, radio show appearances, stage show roles, film options, and teaching positions at major universities. Some of these opportunities would have come their way without the slam's help but many would not have.

The media attention and focus a slam or a slammer receives is often enough to catapult an individual or group of individuals into huge commercial success. Ambitions that were once absurd for a poet to think about now seem very possible. And that's okay as long as their art remains honest and as sacred as it was when there were no worldly temptations to consider. The best to all those slammers who have moved on up, and may they also keep a hand connected to the hands that helped them up.

If you remember anything, remember...

- As slammaster, your job doesn't end when the doors open.
- Greet patrons at the door, introduce them to one another, and make sure they feel welcome before that first performer steps onstage.
- Be prepared to deal with a wide range of personality types, especially when dealing with temperamental performers.
- Start your show on time, end on time, and make sure the audience stays engaged.
- You can add to your show's income and feed fan appetites by selling anthologies, compilation CDs, T-shirts, and other merchandise.
- Don't forget where you got your start and how many hands, heads, and hearts helped you get there.

APPENDIX A
SLAMMERS: PERFORMANCE POETRY

Poetry Collections

Barnidge, Mary Shen. *Piano Player at the Dionysia.* Chicago: Thompson Hill Publishing, 1984.

Brown, Michael. *Falling Wallendas.* Chicago: Tia Chucha Press, 1994.

Buscani, Lisa. *Jangle.* Chicago: Tia Chucha Press, 1992.

Coval, Kevin. *Slingshots.* Channahon, IL: EM Press, 2005.

Fitzpatrick, Tony. *Hard Angels.* Philadelphia, PA: Janet Fleisher Gallery, 1988.

Gillette, Ron. *Hardware & Variety, a collection of poems.* Oak Park, Illinois: Erie Street Press, 1984.

Glazner, Gary Mex. *Ears On Fire: Snapshot Essays In a World of Poets.* Albuquerque, New Mexico: La Alamedia Press, 2002.

Holman, Bob. *A Collect Call of the Wild.* New York: Holt, 1995.

Jess, Tyehimba. *Leadbelly.* Amherst, MA: Verse Press, 2004.

McDaniel, Jeffery. *Alibi School.* San Francisco: Manic D Press, 1995.

McDaniel, Jeffery. *The Endarkenment.* Pittsburgh: University of Pittsburgh Press, 2008.

McDaniel, Jeffery. *The Forgiveness Parade.* San Francisco: Manic D Press, 1998.

McDaniel, Jeffery. *The Splinter Factory.* San Francisco: Manic D Press, 2002.

Moustaki, Nikki. *The Complete Idiot's Guide to Writing Poetry.* Indianapolis: Alpha Books, 2001.

Salach, Cin. *Looking for a Soft Place to Land.* Chicago: Tia Chuca Press, 1996.

Smith, Marc Kelly. *Crowdpleaser.* Chicago: Collage Press, 1996.

Smith, Patricia. *Big Towns, Big Talk.* Hanover, NH: Zoland Books, 2002.

Smith, Patricia. *Blood Dazzler.* Minneapolis: Coffee House Press, 2008.

Smith, Patricia. *Life According to Motown.* Chicago: Tia Chucha Press, 1991.

Smith, Patricia. *Teahouse of the Almighty.* Minneapolis: Coffee House Press, 2006.

West, Phil. *The Arsenal of Small Stars.* Whitmore Lake, MI: The Wordsmith Press, 2005.

Audio & Video Recordings

Bylanzky, Ko and Rayl Patzak. *Europe Speaks, The First European Slam & Spoken Word Poetry Comilation.* Luzern, Switzerland: Verlag Der Gesunde Menschenversand, 2006. www.menchenversand.ch.

Comrade Fatso. *House of Hunger.* Zimbabwe: 2008. www.comradefatso .com.

Devlin, Paul, producer. *Slam Nation. (DVD)* Slammin" Entertainment: 2004. www.slamnation.com.

Eleveld, Mark, ed. *Live at Beyond Baroque 2.* EM Press. Channahon, IL: 2004. www.em-press.com.

Glazner, Gary Mex, director. *Busload of Poets.* PSI: 2000. www.poetryslam .com.

Hacker, Dean, Cin Salach, Marc Smith, and Patricia Smith. *By Someone's Good Grace.* Chicago: Splinter Group engineered by Seth Green, distributed by PSI.

Holman, Bob. *In with the Out Crowd.* New York: MouthAlmighty/ Mercury, 1998.

Kababa, Msandi. *Maswati Lamahle.* Swaziland: Authentic Entertainment: 2008.

Koyczan, Shane. *Perfect.* San Francisco: ReVerb, 1998.

Mali, Taylor. *Poems from the Like Free Zone.* New York: Words Worth Ink, 2000.

Perkins, Chuck. *Voices of the Big Easy.* New Orleans: 2008. www.cdbaby.com.

PSI. *Hear, See, Feel Poetry Slam Inc. (DVD)* Whitmore Lake, MI: 2004. www.poetryslam.com.

PSI. *World's Greatest Poetry Show. (DVD)* PSI: 2003. www.poetryslam.com.

Rorie, David, producer. *Sunday Night Poets. (DVD)* National Film Network: 2002. www.nationalfilmworks.com.

Singh, Chris Mooney. *The Celeletial Voyage.* Singapore: 1998.

TEAM NYC-Urbana 2002, *Urbana.* New York: The Bowery Poetry Club, 2002.

Anthologies

Go to www.poetryslam.com and click on *books* in find a listing of slam anthologies. Below are some of special interest.

Algarin, Miguel and Bob Holman, ed. *ALOUD: Voices from the Nuyorican Poets Café.* New York: Henry Holt and Company, 1994.

Anderton, Luck, Regie Gibson, and Michael Salinger. *From Page to Stage and back Again.* Whitmore Lake, MI: Wordsmith Press/PSI, 2004.

Bylanzky, Ko and Rayl Patsak. *Poetry Slam: Was Die Mikrofone Halten.* Munich, Germany: Posie fur dasneue Jahrtausend. Ariel-Verlag, 2000. (German.)

Bylanzky, Ko and Rayl Patzak. *Planet Slam 2.* Munich, Germany: Yedermann, 2004. (German.)

Eleveld, Mark, ed. *The Spoken Word Revolution.* Naperville, Il: Sourcebooks, 2002.

Eleveld, Mark, ed. *The Spoken Word Revolution Redux*. Naperville, Il: Sourcebooks, 2007.

Glazner, Gary Mex, ed. *Poetry Slam: The Competitive Art of Performance Poetry*. San Francisco: Manic D Press, 2000.

"Gli Ammutinati." Il Volo Del Calabrone. Trieste, Italy: Tipografia Adriatica, 2008. (Italian)

Kaufman, Alan, ed. *The Outlaw Bible of American Poetry*. New York: Thunder's Mouth Press, 1999.

McAllister, Susan, Don McIver, Mikaela Renz, and Daniel S. Solis. *A Bigger Boat—The Unlikely Success of the Albuquerque Poetry Slam Scene*. Albuquerque: University of New Mexico Press, 2008.

Parson-Nesbitt, Julie, Louis J. Rodriguez, and Michael Warr. *Power Lines*. Chicago: Tia Chucha Press, 1999.

Stanton, Victoria and Vincent Tinguely. *Impure: Reinventing the Word*. Montreal, Quebec, Canada: Conundrum Press, 2001.

Publishers of Slam Poetry

The Bowery Poetry Club

308 Bowery
New York City, NY
212–614–1224
www.bowerypoetry.com

EM Press

24041 S. Navajo Dr.
Channahon, IL 60410
www.em-press.com

Manic D Press

Box 410804
San Francisco, CA 94141
info@manicdpress.com
www.manicdpress.com

Rattle Poetry for the 21st Century

12411 Ventura Blvd.
Studio City, CA 91604
www.rattle.com

Sourcebooks

1935 Brookdale Road
Suite 139
Naperville, IL 60563
800–432–7444 (toll-free)
630–961–3900 (phone)
630–961–2168 (fax)
www.sourcebooks.com

Tia Chucha Press

Chicago Distribution Center
11030 South Langley Avenue
Chicago, IL 60628
Tel: 1–800–621–2736 or 312–568–1550
Fax: 1–800–621–8476 or 312–660–2235
www.guildcomplex.com/tiachucha

Agents

If you're turning poet-professional, want a steady stream of gigs, and don't want the hassles of having to negotiate deals, consider hiring an agent to represent you. My slam colleague and confidante Mike McGee (www.MikeMcGee.net) has put together the following list of agents who are well-known in the slam community. According to Mike:

> Here's the top of the heap in Spoken Word. Considering there are hundreds of agencies out there, these are the few that are in any way interested in spoken word or "poetry slammers." There are a few others that are not worth mentioning considering they will not book people they aren't already friends with.

Mudu Multimedia

Walter Mudu is my agent and he likes good entertainers.

Brooklyn, New York

www.mudumultimedia.com

Layman Lyric

Layman Lyric is surely the new kid on the block and doing well. Probably the most bookings for separate poets in the last year.

Houston, Texas

www.laymanlyric.com

Global Talent

I heard from the head of Global Talent that he wasn't much interested in bringing in any new poets, but their spoken word roster is a who's-who of poetry slam.

Manhattan, New York

www.globaltalentassoc.com

The College Agency

Savage, Minnesota

www.thecollegeagency.com

Auburn Moon Agency

Delaware

www.auburnmoonagency.com

APPENDIX B
BOOKS ON POETICS & PERFORMING

Anders, Petra. *Poetry Slam: Live-Poeten in Dichterschlachten Ein Arbeitsbuch*. Muelheim, Germany: Verlag an der Ruhr, 2004. (German)

Blunt, Jerry. *The Composite Art of Acting*. New York: Macmillan Company, 1966.

Bonney, Jo, ed. *Extreme Exposure: An Anthology of Solo Texts from the Twentieth Century*. New York: Theatre Communications Group, 2000.

Duval, Catherine, Laurent Fourcaut, and Pilote Le Hot. *20 ateliers de slam poesie, de l'ecriture petique a la performance*. Paris: Retz, 2008. (French)

Fogler, Janet, and Lynn Stern. *Improving Your Memory*. Baltimore: John Hopkins University Press, 1994.

Foley, John Miles. *How to Read an Oral Poem*. Urbana, IL: University of Illinois Press.

Holbrook, Sara. *Wham! It's a Poetry Jam*. Honesdale, PA: Wordsong/Boyds Mills Press, 2002. (recommended for grade-school children)

Jerome, Judson. *The Poet's Handbook*. Cincinnati: Writer's Digest Books, 1980.

Jesse, Anita. *Let the Part Play You: A Practical Approach to the Actor's Creative Process*. Burbank, CA: Wolf Creek Press, 1994.

Lee, Charlotte I, and Frank Galati. *Oral Interpretation.* Boston: Houghton Mifflin Company, 1977.

Lessac, Arthur. *The Use and Training of the Human Voice: A Practical Approach to Speech and Voice Dynamics.* Mountain View, CA: Mayfield Publishing Company, 1973.

Moore, Sonia. *The Stanislavski System.* New York: Pocket Books/ Viking Press, 1965.

Oliver, Mary. *Rules for the Dance: A Handbook for Writing and Reading Metrical Verse.* New York: Houghton Mifflin Company, 1998.

Padgett, Ron. *The Teachers & Writers Handbook of Poetic Forms.* New York: Teachers & Writers Collaborative, 2000 (second edition).

Parrott, E. O. *How to be Well-versed in Poetry.* London: Penguin Books, 1990.

Stickland, F. Cowles. *The Technique of Acting.* New York: McGraw-Hill, 1956.

Turco, Lewis. *The New Book of Forms: A Handbook of Poetics.* Hanover, NH: University Press of New England, 1986.

APPENDIX C
PSI-CERTIFIED SLAMS

11th Hr Poetry Slam Series (formerly DC Slam)
2021 14th St. NW
Washington, DC 20009
www.dcslam.com

2008 Jackson Hewitt Youth Poetry SummerSlam
1362 NW 54th Street
Miami, FL 33142
tppearson.com

48th St Slam
4814 Chicago Ave S.
Minneapolis, MN 55417
www.slammn.org

7 Deadly Sins Poetry Slam
15th Street (Near College Ave.)
Troy, NY 12180

ABQ Slams

111 Harvard SE
Albuquerque, NM 87102
www.abqslams.org

Accident Slam

210 C St
Eureka, CA 95501
www.myspace.com/areasontolisten

akhristin

2815 South Buffalo Drive
Las Vegas, NV 89117
www.angieb2.com

Ann Arbor Poetry Slam

415 North 1st Street
Richmond, VA 23224
www.myspace.com/SoleilSlam

Ballabajoomba Poetry Slam

505 S. Water Street
Corpus Christi, TX 78401
ballabajoomba.tripod.com

Berkeley Poetry Slam

3101 Shattuck
Berkeley, CA 94704
www.berkeleypoetryslam.com

Boise Poetry Slam Delux at Neurolux

113 N. 11th St.
Boise, ID 83702
www.boisepoetry.com

Boston Poetry Slam @ The Cantab Lounge
738 Massachusetts Ave
Cambridge, MA 02139
www.slamnews.com

Brigham Young University
1 West 2nd South
Rexburg, ID 83440

Broken Speech Poetry Slam
1842 Winter Park Rd
Orlando, FL 32803
brokenspeech.com

ByteThis Poetry & Slam Series
4200 Woodward Avenue
Detroit, MI 48201

City Slam
1519 Mission (at 11th)
San Francisco, CA 94103
www.myspace.com/goldengateslam

Columbia Slam
1009 Gervais Street
Columbia, SC 29201
www.columbiaslam.info

Creative Heat Poetry Slam
Visions Bar & Grill
4263 Moss Street
Lafayette, LA 70507
www.myspace.com/creativeheatpoetryseries

Culture Rapide

103 Rue Julien Lacroix
Paris, France 75020
www.slameur.com

Dallas-Expo Park Café

841 Exposition Ave
Dallas, TX 75226
www.expositionparkcafé.com

Dela Where?—Newark

100 Elkton Rd
Newark, DE 19711
www.delawhere.org

Dela Where—Wilmington

1909 W. 6th Street
Wilmington, DE 19805
www.delawhere.org

Denver-Mercury Slam

2199 California Street
Denver, CO 80205

Denver—slam NUBA!

710 E 26th Ave
Denver, CO 80205
www.myspace.com/slamnuba_team

Detroit EchoVerse Poetry & Slam Series

440 Burroughs St.
Detroit, MI 48202
www.echoversepoetry.com

Detroit Poetry Slam @ The Max!

3711 Woodward Ave

Detroit, MI 48201

Ear Candy: The Normal Poetry Slam

114 E. Beaufort

Normal, IL 61761

www.myspace.com/normalslam

Eclectic Truth Poetry Slam and Open Mic

2857 Perkins Road

Baton Rouge LA 70802

www.xeroskidmore.com

Ending Segregation: "Just Say the Word"

166 E. Bridge St, Homestead

Pittsburgh, PA 15120

www.pittsburghfairhousing.org

First Annual Dubuque Poetry Slam

120 E. 9th St.

Dubuque, IA 52001

www.dbqpoetryslam.com

First Annual Poetry Slam

4913 Weems Street

Moss Point, MS 39563

First Friday Poetry Slam

144 North College Ave.

Fort Collins, CO 80524

www.wolverinefarmpublishing.org/poetrySlam.shtml

FlagSlam

213 S. San Francisco St.
Flagstaff, AZ 86001
www.myspace.com/flagslam

Fourth Friday Poetry Slam

19 Pauahi St.
Honolulu, HI 96813

Friday Night Dallas Poetry Slam

500 North Bishop Avenue
Dallas, TX 75208–4857
www.myspace.com/dallaspoetryslam

FUZE

7133 Germantown Ave
Philadelphia, PA 19140
www.infusioncoffeeandtea.com

Galileo's

2916 N Paseo Dr
Oklahoma City, OK 73103
myspace.com/homeforwaywardpoets

geoff

1080 Joshua Tree Drive
Sierra Vista, AZ 85635

Greater Phoenix Poetry Slam

750 W Grand Ave
Phoenix, AZ 85007
www.anthology.org

Hampshire College Slam Collective

893 West St
Amherst, MA 01002
www.hampshireslam.com

HawaiiSlam

410 Atkinson Drive (ground level in the Ala Moana Hotel)
Honolulu, HI 96814
www.hawaiislam.com

House of Hunger Poetry Slam

Fife Ave and Sixth Street
Harare HRE
2634 Zimbabwe
www.zimbabwearts.co.zw

Houston Poetry Slam

3800 Sherwood Lane
Houston, TX 77092
www.houstonpoetryslam.org

Ithaca Poetry Slam

146 E. State St.
Ithaca, NY 14850
www.slamtractor.com

Jasmine's Poetry Slam

826 3rd Avenue South
Surfside Beach, SC 29575
www.jasminedreams.com

Kalamazoo Poetry Slam
1249 Portage St
Kalamazoo, MI 49002
www.kzooslam.org

Know Wonder $1,000 Poetry Slam
617 Indiana Avenue
Indianapolis, IN 46202
www.know-wonder.org/slam

Knoxville Poetry Slam
842 N. Central St.
Knoxville, TN 37917
www.knoxvillepoetryslam.com

Lapeer Celebrates the Arts Poetry Slam
732 S. Main St.
Almont, MI 48003
www.sunrisekiwanis.com/art.html

Las Vegas Poets Organization
4235 Fairfax Circle #4
Las Vegas, NV 89119
www.lasvegaspoets.org

Legendary Santa Cruz Slam
The Poet and the Patriot
320 Cedar St Ste E.
Santa Cruz, CA 95060
www.santacruzslam.com

Life Sentence

2114 Sutterville Road
Sacramento, CA 95822
www.myspace.com/lifesentenceshow

Loser Slam

765 Newman Springs Rd.
Lincroft, NJ 07738
www.myspace.com/loserslam

Maui Slam at Casanova's

1188 Makawao Avenue
Makawao, HI 96768
www.mauislam.com

Mental Graffiti @ Funky Buddha Lounge

728 W. Grand
Chicago, IL 60610
www.myspace.com/mentalg

Nickel City Poetry Slam

1285 Elmwood Avenue
Buffalo, NY 14222
www.myspace.com/nickelcityslam

Oakland Entirely Poetry Slam

1621 Telegraph Ave
Oakland, CA 94612
www.facebook.com/profile.php?id=589018993

Oakland Primarily Poetry Slam

135 12th St.
Oakland, CA 94607
www.facebook.com/profile.php?id=589018993

Ocotillo Poetry Slam

1730 E Speedway Blvd
Tucson, AZ 85719

Omaha Healing Arts Poetry Slam

1216 Howard Street
Omaha, NE 68102
omahaslam.com

Onomotopeia

300 E. Beecher Street
Bloomington, IL 61701

Poetry Slam

Eureka, CA 95501
www.myspace.com/areasontolisten

Poetry Slam @ the Bridge Café

1117 Elm Street
Manchester, NH 03101
myspace.com/bridgepoetryopenmic

Poetry Slam with Geof Hewitt

Main and School Street
Montpelier, VT 05602
www.kellogghubbard.org

Poets Anonymous K-Zoo

Kalamazoo, MI 49009
www.pakzoo.org

Poets of Clarkston

4915 Pine Knob Lane
Clarkston, MI 48346

PuroSlam

1902 McCollough
San Antonio, TX 78212
www.puroslam.com

rejavanate

3300 East Flamingo
Las Vegas, NV 89121
www.rejavanatecoffee.com

Rhyme Or Die

702 Elms Road
Killeen, TX 76542
killeenpoetryslam.com

Salt City Slam

353 West 200 South
Salt Lake City, UT 84101
www.myspace.com/saltcityslam

San Jose Poetry Slam

510 S. First Street
San Jose, CA 95113
www.maclaarte.org

Sand Slam

739 W Avenue A
Aransas, TX 78373

Scottsdale Poetry Slam

1330 North Scottsdale Road
Scottsdale, AZ 85257
www.anthology.org

Seattle Poetry Slam

513 N. 36th St.
Seattle, WA 98103
www.seattlepoetryslam.org

Second Tuesday Slam

225 Congress St
Portland, ME 04101
www.portveritas.org

Silver City Slam

202 North Bullard
Silver City, NM 88061
www.silvercityslam.com

Slamarillo

3701 Plains Blvd
Amarillo, TX 79102
www.slamarillo.com

SlamCharlotte

345 N. College Street
Charlotte, NC 28202
www.slamcharlotte.com

Slam Dada

2720 Elm St
Dallas, TX 75226
www.slamdada.com

Slammin' on Main

2701 Bearcat Way
Cincinnati, OH 45221–0220
www.uc.edu/mainstreet/tuc/tuc_catskeller.html

SlamMN

330 2nd Ave S.
Minneapolis, MN 55403
www.myspace.com/slamminnesota

Slam Nahuatl presents "The End Hunger Slam"

200 W. Marshall Street (Gallery 5)
Richmond, VA 23220
www.myspace.com/slamnahuatl

Slam Richmond

0 E 4th Street
Richmond, VA 23224
www.myspace.com/slamrichmondslamteam

SlamRichmond

ArtSpace Gallery, Zero E. 4th St.
Richmond, VA 23224
www.myspace.com/slamrichmond

Slam Wars

7118 Mount Royal Ave.
Westerville, OH 43082

Soleil Slam

415 North 1st Street
Richmond, VA 23224
www.myspace.com/SoleilSlam

speakeasie

340 King Rd.
Jacksonville, NC 28540
speakeasie.com

Springfield Library Poetry Slam

220 State Street
Springfield, MA 01108
springfieldlibrary.org/poetry/poetrypage.html

Star City Slam

1624 South Street
Lincoln, NE 68503 US
www.myspace.com/lincolnslam

Steel City Slam

5972 Baum Boulevard
Pittsburgh, PA 15206

St. Louis Poetry SLAM!

2720 Sutton
St. Louis, MO 63143

S.Y.M Poetry Slam

405 South 5 Street
Reading, PA 19602

Upstate Carolina Slam

1 East Coffee Street
Greenville, SC 29601
www.witsendpoetry.com

Uptown Poetry Slam

4802 N. Broadway
Chicago, IL 60640
slampapi.com

Urbana

308 Bowery
New York City, NY 10012
www.bowerypoetry.com/urbana

Ursa Major Poetry Slam

409 W Big Bear Blvd
Big Bear City, CA 92314
ursamajorpoetry.wordpress.com

Vancouver Poetry Slam

2096 Commercial Drive
Vancouver, BC
V6A 2B1 Canada
www.vancouverpoetryhouse.com

Vermillion Literary Project

24 W. Main Street
Vermillion, SD 57069
www.usd.edu/orgs/projlit

Vibe Session

75 Public Square
Cleveland, OH 44113
www.chiefrocka.com

Worcester Poets' Asylum

1073A Main St.
Worcester, MA 01603
poetsasylum.org

WORD UP!

Sofienstraße 12
Heidelberg Ba-Wu
69115 Germany
www.wordup-hd.de

Writers' Block Poetry Night

2250 N. High St.
Columbus, OH 43201
www.writersblockpoetry.com

ZorkSlam @ White Plains Library

100 Martin Ave.
White Plains, NY 10605
www.stolensnapshots.com

GET ON STAGE AND PERFECT YOUR PERFORMANCE

Have you ever enjoyed a slam or two and thought, "I could do this," but felt apprehensive staring at that empty mic—or worse, you climbed up on stage and struggled?

Let Marc Kelly Smith, the founder of Slam Poetry, teach you everything you need to be a confident performer, from writing a powerful poem, to stage techniques, to going on tour (if that's where your muse leads you).

Take the Mic is filled with insider tips, backstage advice, and tons of examples of slam poems that wake up an audience. With this book, you'll also be able to link to the PoetrySpeaks.com community to listen to samples, meet poets, and unearth inspirations for your next performance.

ABOUT THE AUTHORS

Marc Kelly Smith is the creator and founder of the International Poetry Slam movement. As stated in the PBS television series *The United States of Poetry*, a "strand of new poetry began at Chicago's Green Mill Tavern in 1987 when Marc Smith found a home for the Poetry Slam." Since then, performance poetry has spread throughout the world, exported to more than five hundred cities large and small.

Chalking up more than two thousand engagements in nightclubs, concert halls, libraries, universities—and on top of the occasional hot dog stand—Marc continues to entertain and inspire audiences as diverse and eager as any to be found in the realm of fine arts. He has performed at the Kennedy Center, the Smithsonian Institute, Galway's Cruit Festival, Denmark's Roskilde Festival, Ausburg's ABC Brecht Festival, and the Queensland Poetry Fest in Australia. He has hosted over one thousand standing-room-only shows at the Green Mill's original slam and has been featured on CNN, *60 Minutes*, and National Public Radio. He narrated the Sourcebooks releases *Spoken Word Revolution* and *Spoken Word Revolution Redux*. Marc's volume of poetry, *Crowdpleaser* (Collage Press), and his CDs, *It's About Time*, *Quarters in the Juke Box*, and *Love & Politics*, are available through his website, www.slampapi.com.

Joe Kraynak is a professional writer who has authored and co-authored numerous books, including *The Complete Idiot's Guide to Computer Basics*, *Flipping Houses for Dummies*, *Food Allergies for Dummies*, *Bipolar Disorder for Dummies*, and *Master Visually: Optimizing Your PC*. Joe graduated from Purdue University in 1982 with a bachelor's degree in creative writing and philosophy and again in 1984 with a master's degree in English literature. In the summer of 2003, Mikal Belicove, acquisitions editor for *The Complete Idiot's Guide to Slam Poetry*, introduced Marc and Joe, catalyzing the birth of a creative dynamo. Joe attended his first slam at the 2003 nationals in Chicago, where he and his wife, Cecie, served as judges. For more about Joe, visit his blog at JoeKraynak.com.